BONUS FEATURE

How To Memorize Scripture:

Social Media:

RANDELLHOLMESJR

*This book is dedicated to my parents.
Mom, Dad, thank you. I wouldn't be the
man I am today without y'all.*

DAY 1

"I chose you."

- John 15:16

DAILY DEVOTIONAL

It is crucial that you know you are destined to do great things for God. Just as Jesus chose his disciples, God also chose you to follow and live for him. It says in Psalm 139:13, "For you formed my inward parts; you knitted me together in my mother's womb." Before you could ever choose God, he already knew you and chose you because he loves you.

However, it is also important for you to choose God. See it this way: the God of the universe chose YOU to change your life for the good and advance his kingdom, but you have to choose to follow God and make him the Savior of your life. If you follow the Lord, your life will have a purpose and meaning that nothing else can give you.

There are still many people out there who are not saved and have not chosen God. 2 Peter 3:9 tells us, "The Lord is not slow to fulfill his promise as some count slowness, but patient toward you, not wishing that any should perish but that all should reach repentance." People often ask, "Why can't God just save everyone?" Since God is a loving God, he gives us free will. This means we have the chance to make a decision.

God, being the loving God he is, will not force anyone's decision. He wants all to choose him, but he understands that some will not, and he respects that. God simply gives every person what

DAY 1

they choose. If you choose God, God honors your choice, and you get to be in the presence of the Lord for all eternity. If you decide not to choose God, God honors your choice, and you will be separated from God for all eternity.

Another common question is, "Why doesn't God come back already and fix this?"

The moment Jesus comes back for the second time is when judgment will take place, and our eternities will be determined. God desires everyone to come to know him, so he is patient to return. That way, more and more people can have the chance to choose him.

DAILY DO

Have you chosen to follow God?

If yes, pray that others who do not know God will come to know him and choose him.

If not, what's holding you back? Say this prayer to God if you mean it: "God, thank you for loving me and choosing me despite how many times I have sinned. Lord, please forgive me of my sins and give me a new heart. I need a Savior, God, and I need you. Choosing sin will never satisfy me, but choosing you will satisfy and give my life purpose. God, I believe in you. I believe you sent your Son, Jesus, to die and rise again. So, God, I choose you. I choose to make you the Lord and the Savior of my life. I choose to follow you with all my heart."

"No one can serve two masters."

– Matthew 6:24

DAILY DEVOTIONAL

In the book of Matthew, Jesus teaches his disciples that "no one can serve two masters; he will either hate one and love the other or be loyal to one and despise the other." Then he added, "You cannot serve God and money." Money is a reference to the physical things of this world. But it really means anything that takes the place of God in a man's heart.

In the Old Testament, the Israelites once thought they could serve God and an idol named Baal. But in the sight of God, worshiping an idol other than God is an act of betrayal because human hearts cannot be loyal to two masters.

We can apply this to today by asking ourselves, "What do I love most?" Do you love playing video games more than you love God?

God is concerned with where your heart is. What has ownership of your life? It is tough to love God more than the things of this world, but something to know is the things of this world will fade. To prove this, let me ask you a question. Think back to last Christmas. Was there a present that you wanted really bad, and you got it? Now, let me ask this. Do you still use that present as much as you did whenever you got it on Christmas?

Would you rather love something that one day will not be there or love something that will never leave your side? This is why we are to surrender our lives to God and serve him because he will never fade or leave our side. We were all created by God and for God. Therefore, our lives should be in total service to our creator. Belonging to God means belonging to everything he stands for: holiness, righteousness, faith, joy, peace, mercy, kindness, gentleness, etc.

DAILY DO

Ask yourself, "Who do I belong to?" Pray that God will help you let go of any other masters you are following. Ask God to make your heart and desires be directed towards him.

"Set your minds on things above, not earthly things."

- Colossians 3:2

DAILY DEVOTIONAL

The things here on earth are temporary. They do not last forever, whereas the things in heaven are eternal—they last forever and ever. As children of God, our real home is in heaven, and one day, we will dwell there for all eternity. The things of this earth cannot and will not go to heaven with us. You cannot take your clothes, shoes, or car to heaven.

This is why Scripture teaches us to seek heavenly things over earthly things. In the book of Luke, there is a story of a man called the "Rich, Young Ruler." In this story, we see a very wealthy man. This man loves his money so much that when Jesus asks him to give it to the poor, he is unable to because he loves his wealth too much. He was setting his mind on money and not heavenly things.

This story took place 2,000 years ago, but there are 3 things that we know about the rich, young ruler today.

The rich, young ruler…

1. is no longer rich

2. is no longer young

3. and he isn't ruling over anything now

DAY 3

So many people prefer money, fame, and power over a relationship with God. But money, fame, and power will mean nothing to you when you are in heaven.

If you want to fix your heart and mind on things above, you have to change your desires to things above. Some good ways to set your mind on things above are to pray, sing worship songs, and study God's word. All these things are pleasing to God.

DAILY DO

Write down one thing you struggle to set your mind on instead of Christ. Pray that God would help you not get distracted by the worldly things around you. Desire the things that God desires. Remember, earth is the journey, and heaven is the goal.

DAY 4

*"Every word of God proves true; he is a
shield to those who take refuge in him."*

DAILY DEVOTIONAL

Why is the word of God important and powerful? 2 Timothy 3:16
tells us that "All Scripture is God-**breathed**." And check this
out—Genesis 2:7 says, "God formed the man of dust from the
ground and **breathed** into his nostrils the **breath** of life, and the
man became a living creature."

If you are not making the connection, I'll help you make it. The
same breath of God that God breathed into Adam when he made
him resides in the very pages of your Bible. When you open your
Bible and read it, you are being filled with the breath of God.

That is why God's word is so important and powerful. God's
word is pure and holy; his promises are true and never fail. God's
word is a shield to those who believe and read it.

God created the heavens and the earth by his word. He said, "Let
there be light," and there was light. He continued to speak until
all things were fully formed. If his word is that powerful, imagine
how much his word can bring light and transformation to your
life.

DAILY DO

Read the first chapter of the book of Genesis. Recognize how powerful God's word is.

DAY 5

"Before I formed you in the womb, I knew you."

- Jeremiah 1:5

DAILY DEVOTIONAL

God already knew you before you were ever born. Can you believe that? Isn't that incredible?

God already chose you and knew who he wanted you to become before your mom and dad knew you. This means you are beyond precious to God. You have always belonged to him. God's love for you is unconditional, which means nothing you can do will make God love you more, and nothing you do will make God love you less. He loves you simply because you are his son.

DAILY DO

Say this prayer to God: "Thank you, Lord, for creating me in your image; thank you for the plans you have for me. Help me to live for you for all of the days of my life. Amen."

"God saved you by his grace when you believed. And you can't take credit for this; it is a gift from God."

- Ephesians 2:8

DAILY DEVOTIONAL

Imagine there was a 16-year-old boy named Luke. One day, Luke was speeding and got pulled over by a police officer. The officer issued Luke a ticket for $300. Luke does not have a job. He cannot pay for the ticket, and, therefore, he has to go to court. A few days later, Luke goes to court to attempt to settle the conflict. When Luke enters the courtroom, he sees that the judge is his dad. Luke knew his father was a judge, but he did not expect him to be the judge of his case. Luke tells his father that he knows what he did was wrong. He went over the speed limit, which is against the law, but he does not have the money to pay the punishment. Rather than sending his son to jail, the judge said, "Luke, my son, I know you cannot pay this debt. But because I love you and want to show mercy, I will cleanse you of your debt. You no longer owe $300. However, even though I am a merciful judge, I am also a fair and just judge. This is why the $300 cannot just go unpaid. Someone has to pay the consequences of your actions. As a result, I will pay for your ticket. I will take the debt that you deserve."

This is very similar to how God loves and shows mercy to us. We are in debt to Jesus. We have all sinned. According to Romans 6:23, "The wages of sin is death." The punishment of sin is separation from Christ, but since he loves you so dearly, he cleanses you of your debt. Jesus did this by living a perfect life

DAY 6

and dying on the cross so that you and I do not have to. That is grace. That is true love.

DAILY DO

Write down three specific things you are thankful for. Tell Jesus how grateful you are for him dying on the cross for your sins.

DAY 7

"Instead of each person watching out for their own good, watch out for what is better for others."

- Philippians 2:4

DAILY DEVOTIONAL

Selflessness is one of the best characteristics you can develop as a Christian. It even says in Matthew 20:16, "So the last will be first, and the first last." This means those who aim to put others before themselves will be rewarded in heaven. Jesus showed incredible selflessness when he died on the cross. I can assure you Jesus did not want to die. We even read in Matthew 26:39 that Jesus cried out to God, "My Father, if it is possible, let this cup pass from me; nevertheless not as I will, but as you will." Notice how Jesus says, "Not as I will, but as you will." He is putting God the Father's will and desire before his own.

We live in a world where some people's goal is to have people serve them. Can you remember a time in your life when you used someone to serve you? As people gain more power and wealth, they expect to hold more equity or standing among others. Take worldly kings and leaders, for example. They expect to be served. Yet, Jesus, the King of Kings and the greatest leader to ever walk the face of the earth, did not come to be served but came to serve others. Jesus humbled himself to take on the form of a servant. That's incredible.

Please know this does not mean you should not care for yourself. Rather, you are showing the same care for others as you desire to be shown to you.

DAILY DO

Decide to put someone's needs before yours today. It could be your brother, sister, parents, or friend. Remember this:

- God 1st
- Others 2nd
- I'm 3rd

DAY 8

DAILY DEVOTIONAL

It can be hard to understand how the Trinity works. There are three different persons/entities, but they are all the same God:

1. God the Father

2. Jesus

3. The Holy Spirit

All three entities are God but are different persons and serve different purposes.

- God the Father created all and made all. He resides in heaven.

- Jesus is the Son of God who came to earth to save us from our sins and now resides in heaven at the right hand of God the Father.

- The Holy Spirit is what God has granted us so that we may have communion with God and the Spirit of God in us.

The Holy Spirit that God granted us resides in us once we accept Jesus as our Lord and Savior. This Spirit that God has gifted us with is the Spirit of God, so since you have the Spirit of God, you also now have God's power, love, and self-discipline inside you.

DAY 8

The Spirit convicts us when we do wrong. It gives us discernment, wisdom, and counsel for hard decisions. It gives us strength and fortitude to do hard things. It intercedes for us when we are weak (Romans 8:26-27).

Notice how none of the things the Spirit gives us include fear or timidness. Once you believe in God, you have the Spirit of God inside you, so any emotion/thought that is not like God or of God is not from God. God does not give you fear or timidness; that is something our sinful nature has brought upon us. God sees you. God knows you. God loves you. And, the Spirit of the living God dwells inside of your body. Since the Spirit of God empowers us, you are not to be someone who gives up in the face of challenges; you are a powerful child of God who can climb up every mountain or tackle any problem that life throws at you.

DAILY DO

Write down this Scripture somewhere in your journal, on your mirror, or in a place where you will see it often, and confess it over your life, "For God has not given me the spirit of fear, but of power, of love, and a sound mind." (2 Timothy 1:7)

DAY 9

"For we are His workmanship, created in Christ Jesus for good works, which God prepared beforehand that we should walk in them."

- Ephesians 2:10

DAILY DEVOTIONAL

A potter molds clay into a shape or a form he desires it to become. He keeps on shaping it until it is perfect. Even though we will never be perfect on this side of heaven, God is also a potter, and you are his clay. He longs to mold you into the shape he desires, and I don't mean the size and shape of your body but of your mind, life, and destiny. God didn't save you just so you can go to heaven. Yes, God wants you to go to heaven, but he also wants to make something beautiful out of you right now! Even at a young age, God wants to use you in amazing ways. The word "workmanship" means "work of art." That means we are God's beautiful artwork. That is just so amazing to hear, right? You are a masterpiece that God is carefully composing.

Submit your life to God. Let him take control and work on your heart because he will make something beautiful out of you.

DAILY DO

Listen to the song "Nothing I Hold on To" by Will Reagan, and thank God for sending his Son to die for your sins.

DAY 10

"So do not fear, for I am with you; do not be dismayed, for I am your God. I will strengthen you and help you; I will uphold you with my righteous right hand."

- Isaiah 41:10

DAILY DEVOTIONAL

Have you ever been scared? Maybe you were worried about something that was going to be difficult. Or perhaps you were scared to do something you were not used to? In the Scripture above, God commands the Israelites not to fear even though their city was destroyed and the Babylonians ruled over them. This was something the Israelites were not used to. They were God's chosen people, but at this point, they probably did not feel like God's chosen people because of their circumstances.

However, we know how the story ends. Ultimately, God delivers his people, and Jesus comes to be the Savior of the world. God commands his people not to fear because he will "strengthen them" and "uphold them," and even though God said this to the Israelites some 2500 years ago, it applies to us because he says a similar thing to you in 2 Timothy 1:7. There it says, "for God gave us a spirit not of fear but of power, love, and self-control." You do not have to fear because you have God on your side. You have God's power and love in you, which is enough to overcome any hard or scary thing in your life. Just as God protected his chosen people, the Israelites, thousands of years ago, he will protect you because, remember, from **DAY 1**, God chose you.

DAY 10

The God we follow today is the same God from the Old Testament. He protected his people then, and he will protect you now.

DAILY DO

Repeat the words "I _____(say your name), will not fear, for God is with me. He will strengthen me and hold me with his mighty hand."

DAY 10
CHECK IN

DAY 11

"If we confess our sins, he will forgive our sins."

- 1 John 1:9

DAILY DEVOTIONAL

Confession is a sign of remorse and recognition you have done wrong. When your parents ask you to clean your room, and you do not, that is disobedience. You have done something wrong that you need to confess. When you confess to your mom and dad, you tell them what you did and that you are sorry for your disobedience.

By doing so, you humble yourself; you show your parents that you are genuinely sorry and realize an area you can improve.

The same is true for God. When we confess our sins, we are humbling ourselves before God and showing him that we are truly sorry. We are pointing out an area of our lives that we need to be better in.

Perhaps sometimes, after you sin, you may not feel worthy to even talk to him. After your sin, you might feel like God doesn't want you around unless you're perfect. It's actually quite the opposite: God wants you to run to him whenever you sin. He's the type of loving father who will welcome you with open arms no matter what you do.

You do not have to be perfect. You do not have to make yourself better before you run to God. God wants you exactly where you are at this very moment. Run to him now and let him love, comfort, and make you a better person.

David, in the Bible, was a man who knew how forgiving God was. He always ran to God when he made terrible mistakes, and God continuously forgave him. God saw this in David and blessed him. David is known in the Bible as "a man after God's own heart."

What's holding you back from being a man after God's own heart?

*** Do know that when you confess and apologize, make sure you are not just repeating the same mistake over and over; be sincere about changing for good.

DAILY DO

1. Confess your sins.
2. Be sincere.
3. Run to the arms of the Father and let him help you overcome your sin.
4. Be a man after God's own heart.

DAY 12

"For everyone who calls on the name of the Lord will be saved."

- Romans 10:13

DAILY DEVOTIONAL

If you are reading this, you have been reading this devotional consistently, and I'm proud of you! You have probably read the phrase "You are a child of God" or "son of God" multiple times.

Today, I want to give you a chance to become a "child of God" in case you are not already. We did something very similar on DAY 1.

But I would love to ask you this question again because it is the most important question you'll ever answer in your entire life: are you saved?

This simply means, have you surrendered your life to Jesus and chosen to make him your Lord and Savior? You can do this simply by calling upon his name, letting go of your sins, and believing in him. Romans 10:9 says: "If you **confess** with your mouth the Lord Jesus and **believe** in your heart that God raised him from the dead, you will be saved." Two keywords in this Scripture are **confess** and **believe**.

It starts with **confession**. Do you agree that you are sinful? That you cannot save yourself and you are in need of a Savior? If so, confess your sin. Recognize you are not capable of salvation by yourself. See that you are dependent on Jesus for salvation.

Then you have to **believe**. Do you believe that the power and righteousness of Jesus is enough to save you? Do you believe that Jesus died for you and defeated the grave three days later, something that no man has ever done before? Do you genuinely believe these things in your heart?

So, I'll ask again: are you saved? Being saved sets you **free** from the power of sin—you become a child of God.

DAILY DO

You must be wondering how to do all I said above. If you genuinely want to make Jesus the Lord of your life, pray this aloud: "Lord Jesus, I believe you died on the cross for me to be saved from sin and death. Forgive me of all my sins. I confess that you alone are God and that I depend on you. I accept you into my life today to become my Lord and Savior. I love you, Lord. Thank you for saving me. Amen."

If you said those prayers for the first time, congratulations! Heaven rejoices over you right now! Because you just became a child of God! If this is a prayer you have already prayed and God is already the Lord of your life, that is great! Continue to follow the Lord and tell your friends about him so they can also become children of God!

DAY 13

"For the things which are seen are temporary, but the things which are not seen are eternal."

- 2 Corinthians 4:18

DAILY DEVOTIONAL

I want you to imagine a really, really long rope. A rope that never ends. On that rope, I want you to imagine a piece of red tape about maybe 6 inches. The really, really long rope represents eternity. The 6 inches of red tape represent your life on earth. We cannot see eternity now because we are here on earth, and here on earth, our lives are temporary. Our life is in the 6 inches of red tape compared to the really, really long rope that has no end. We may not be able to see eternity now, but it is coming. Will you live your life for this life and what's temporary, or will you live your life for the next life and what is eternal?

DAILY DO

Watch this video by Francis Chan, posted by Nate Hanson.

"So encourage each other and build each other up."

- 1 Thessalonians 5:11

DAILY DEVOTIONAL

The Bible teaches us to encourage and to build each other up as a family in Christ. We are to knit our hearts together with one goal and one mission—to bring glory to God and advance his kingdom. David writes in Psalms 133:1, "How good and pleasant it is when brothers dwell together in unity." How are we supposed to be united in Christ if we are divisive and tearing each other down? Therefore, encourage one another and remind one another of his word. Hebrews 4:12 says, "The word of God is living and active, sharper than any two-edged sword piercing to the division of soul and of spirit." The word of God pierces division. The Bible is the greatest resource to encourage and unite us brothers and sisters in Christ.

DAILY DO

If you see someone feeling down, encourage them with the word of God, bring a smile to their face, and give them hope.

DAY 15

"Don't be defeated by evil, but defeat evil with good."

- Romans 12:21

DAILY DEVOTIONAL

When Jesus was poorly treated, beaten, spat on, mocked, laughed at, and nailed to the cross, it only made sense for him to defend himself by calling down mighty angels to avenge him, right? He is God; he has the power to do so, but he didn't. He chose not to repay evil with evil. Instead, he repaid evil with good. He gave them grace, love, and his life in return for the evil done to him.

We are commanded in Matthew 5 to "love our enemies and pray for those who persecute us." That is what Jesus did for us. Jesus died for us even though we are still sinners.

To repay evil for evil is like fighting a fire with more fire. A fire only cools down when water is sprayed on it. Water is the complete opposite substance of fire. Whereas fire is hot, water is cool, and because of that, it suppresses the flames. But if you were to try to suppress one fire with another fire, it would just make an even bigger fire.

In the same way, why do we expect that being mean, angry, and rude to those who are mean, angry, and rude to us will make the situation any better? To fight evil with evil will only escalate the situation. Therefore, do not fight evil with evil, but fight it with good.

DAY 15

Choose to love, choose to be friendly, and choose to say kind words to people no matter if they are nice to you or not. Dare to be different, just like Jesus was.

DAILY DO

Is there someone you know that isn't nice to you? Say a warm "hello" to them this week, give them a small gift, and tell them that Jesus loves them. Don't worry about their reply or reaction. Just know by doing so, your heavenly Father is proud of you!

DAY 16

"The Lord bless you and keep you. The Lord makes his face shine upon you and be gracious to you."

- Numbers 6:24

DAILY DEVOTIONAL

God constantly desires to bless his children; his blessings bring goodness, prosperity, success, joy, and peace. Who doesn't want these things?

The more we draw closer to God, the more his blessings get poured out on us. This doesn't mean you are promised an easier life, more money, more popularity, etc. The blessings that will be poured on you will be blessings of peace, confidence, love, joy, and the gifts of God. It may be hard to honestly believe this, but I promise you the things God can bless you with are far better than what the world can give you. God wants to give you his blessing. He wants to provide you with his comfort and freedom from the chains and lies of sin.

Don't be afraid to ask for blessings from the Lord. He wants to give them to you. Matthew 7:7-11 proves this: "Ask, and it will be given to you; seek, and you will find; knock, and it will be opened to you. For everyone who asks receives, and the one who seeks find, and to the one who knocks it will be opened. Or which one of you, if his son asks for bread, will give him a stone? Or if he asks for a fish, will give him a serpent? If you then, who are evil, know how to give good gifts to your children, how much more will your Father who is in heaven give good things to those who ask him!"

DAY 16

Practice asking the Lord for blessings. How long it takes or how God blesses you may not always look how you want, but God knows best and will bless you at the proper time.

DAILY DO

Listen to the song "The Blessing" by Kari Jobe, Cody Carnes, and Elevation Worship. Ask the Lord to bless you, keep you, and have his face shine upon you.

DAY 17

*"In the beginning, God created the heavens
and the earth."*

- Genesis 1:1

DAILY DEVOTIONAL

Many people are filled with questions about the existence of God. Some ask, "Is God real?" Others ask, "Who made God?"

You do not have to bother your mind with questions like that because the answer is in the very first verse of the entire Bible. Anything that is created needs a creator. A watch requires a watchmaker. A computer needs a machine that assembles it. A painting needs a painter to paint it. So if our world was created, it needs a creator, and that creator is God.

But you may ask, "If everything needs a creator, who created God?" You see, God is eternal, that means everlasting. God was never created because he has always existed and always will exist. That is why God calls himself "I AM THAT I AM." He is the beginning and the end of all things; he existed before anything began and will continue to exist for all eternity.

So, to answer the two most commonly asked questions:

1. Is God real? Yes, God is real because the earth was created, which means it needs a creator. God is that creator.

2. Who created God? No one created God. God is God. He has always existed, and everything exists because of him—humans, the earth, heaven, etc.

DAY 17

You come from this mighty God who calls you his own. Isn't that the greatest blessing ever? Take pride that God created you and bless the Lord with the life he has blessed you with!

DAILY DO

Read Genesis 1 and imagine how great, how beautiful, and how powerful God is to have created you, to have created the world, and to have created the entire universe!

DAY 18

"The LORD knows the way of the righteous,
but the way of the wicked will perish."

- Psalm 1:6

DAILY DEVOTIONAL

As Christians, we are to strive to be righteous, holy, and blameless. While we are to strive to be righteous, we will never be wholly righteous, and we will never be perfect because we are human. So do not hold yourself to the standard of perfection; however, what God wants from you is a perfect effort!

To walk in righteousness is a sign that you are walking with God; if you are walking with God, your life will be better than if you are not.

What does it mean to walk in righteousness? What does it mean to walk in the way of the wicked?

To walk in the way of the wicked means you are living unrighteously or sinfully. When you sin, you are saying, "God, I know what I am doing is wrong, but I'm going to do it anyway because it's what I want."

But if you walk in righteousness, that means you are trying to live as purely and holy as possible. In order to walk in righteousness, you must submit your desires to God. No matter how badly you may want to sin in a moment, you will decide not to because walking with God is so much better than walking without him.

DAY 18

DAILY DO

Talk to your parents about some sins you struggle with. Ask them to help you and hold you accountable to walk on the path of righteousness.

DAY 19

"Let all that you do be done with love."

- 1 Corinthians 16:14

DAILY DEVOTIONAL

When Jesus was asked what the greatest commandment was in Matthew 22:37-40, he responded with, "You shall love the Lord your God with all your heart and with all your soul and with all your mind. This is the first and greatest commandment. And a second is like it. You shall love your neighbor as yourself. On these two commandments depend all the Law and the Prophets." To put it in the simplest terms possible, We are to love God and love people.

This should be our aim in life! More than anything else, God is concerned with us loving him and loving those made in his image.

There is another story in Matthew 25:40 where Jesus says, "Truly, I say to you, as you did it to one of the least of these my brothers, you did it to me." Jesus is saying that when you show love to others, you are also showing love to God. Every time you smile at someone, you smile at God. Every time you compliment someone, you compliment God. Every time you help someone in need, you help God. One of the easiest and most practical ways to love God is to love others.

At the end of the day, we are called to love others because God loved us first.

DAY 19

DAILY DO

Have you told someone you love them today? If not, do so. After you tell them, do something for them that shows your love for them.

DAY 20

"Jesus Christ is the same yesterday, today, and forever."

- Hebrews 13:8

DAILY DEVOTIONAL

God is an unchanging God, which means Jesus is an unchanging Jesus. The same person Jesus was 2,000 years ago is the same person he is today and will be forever.

Some people think that since Jesus isn't physically walking on the earth today, God's love, will, and plan have changed. We follow an eternal and unchanging God. The God that we read about in the Old Testament that created the heavens and the earth is the same God that we read about in the New Testament and is the same God that created you. The Jesus that died on the cross 2,000 years ago is the same Jesus that sits at the right hand of the Father in heaven. The Spirit that raised Jesus from the dead is the same Spirit that is alive and in you.

God is unchanging. His word is unchanging. People try to change the rules when God hasn't.

God says he will never leave you nor forsake you. This promise lasts forever because God lasts forever.

DAILY DO

Let the words of Jesus guide you today, tomorrow, and forever. Write down one thing you love about God and thank him for being unchanging.

> *"Thus says the Lord to you, 'Do not be afraid and do not be dismayed at this great [trouble], for the battle is not yours but God's."*

- 2 Chronicles 20:15

DAILY DEVOTIONAL

The context of this verse is that the Israelites were confronted by their enemies, the Moabites and the Ammonites. They were vastly outnumbered, and because of that, the Israelites had very little confidence that they would win the battle. Suddenly, the Spirit of God came upon a young man named Jahaziel, and the words above were spoken to Jahaziel. This gave peace and confidence to the Israelites, and they were assured that God would fight the battle for them, as he had said before.

In life, you will have your own battles. Life is hard, but God uses battles to make us stronger. James 1:2-3 tells us, "Consider it joy when you encounter trials of various kinds, knowing that the testing of your faith produces steadfastness." This means to have joy when hard times come because they will strengthen you.

Also, be at peace because you are not fighting this battle alone. You are also fighting a battle that has already been won. God has your back, and he always will. All we can do is bow down in worship and gratitude that the Lord is our defender.

Every trial in your life, every battle you face, and every person you think is an enemy will one day bow to the God who stands by you. Your fight is his fight. How amazing is it that we serve a God who fights our battles?

DAY 21

DAILY DO

Listen and worship to the songs "Defender" by Francesca Battistelli and "Surrounded (Fight My Battles)" by Upperroom.

Defender

Surrounded (Fight My Battles)

DAY 22

"Children, obey your parents in the Lord, for this is right."

- Ephesians 6:1

DAILY DEVOTIONAL

Mom and Dad often tell you what to do. My parents often told me to clean my room, to have good manners around others, or that I couldn't hang with my friends until I did my homework. Do you know why your parents do this? Because they love you and are training you to follow the path that God wants for you.

God has commanded your mom and dad to teach you how to live a life following the Lord. Your parents are trying to build you up so you can use your gifts and abilities to glorify God.

You do not always know what is best for you, but your mom and dad do because they are older and wiser. God has placed them in your life to lead you well. As their son, you must learn to trust God and obey your parents. They want what is best for you.

At the same time, your parents are human too. They are bound to have their imperfections and shortcomings. Be gracious and forgiving towards them, and it will be easier to follow them.

DAILY DO

Tell your parents you love and are thankful for them, even when you fail to obey or respect them.

DAY 23

> *"For people this is impossible. But for God all things are possible."*

- Mark 10:27

DAILY DEVOTIONAL

There are many things that are impossible for men to do, such as walking on water, healing incurable diseases, and resurrecting from the dead. What's incredible is that Jesus did all these things and more!

Have you ever imagined how your body, the earth, or the universe were formed? These things were made possible only by God. Scientists can explain so little that even they admit that there are occurrences that are beyond scientific explanation.

When it comes to the problems and challenges in the world today, we can question God's sovereignty. We question if God is really in control. Sometimes, we see people who curse God, and we can never imagine them being saved. But God says nothing is too difficult for him. The man who rebukes God could be the same man whose heart radically changes for God and one day becomes a preacher. A man who once rebuked God can be the same man who is redeemed and delivered. There are many people with a similar story. One example from the Bible is a man named Paul. A man who once cursed and hated God became the same man who wrote half of the New Testament.

Never think anything is impossible for God. Never believe that anyone is incapable of being saved. Never give up on a non-believer because God is all-powerful, and his will *will* be done.

DAY 23

DAILY DO

Ask God to do something in your life that only he can do. Remember to stay in faith no matter what you and your family may be going through!

DAY 24

"Clothe yourselves with humility toward each other. God stands against the proud, but he gives favor to the humble."

- 1 Peter 5:5

DAILY DEVOTIONAL

Humility is one of the greatest virtues you could have as a child of God. Do you have friends who love to brag about themselves? How does that make you feel when they boast and brag to your face? Or maybe you are guilty of bragging about things you have to others.

We are to be humble because Jesus Christ was humble. The only man who ever had a right to brag humbled himself before the Lord. Not only are we to humble ourselves before God but also to others. The Bible tells us this explicitly in Philippians 2:3-8: "Do nothing from selfish ambition or conceit, but in humility count others more significant than yourselves. Let each of you look not only to his own interests but also to the interests of others. Have this mind among yourselves, which is yours in Christ Jesus, who though he was in the form of God, did not count equality with God a thing to be grasped, but emptied himself by taking the form of a servant, being born in the likeness of men. And being found in human form, he humbled himself by becoming obedient to the point of death, even death on a cross."

It also tells us in Matthew 23:12, "Whoever exalts himself will be humbled, and whoever humbles himself will be exalted."

So we see repeatedly in Scripture the importance of humility, and

DAY 24

we should want to be humble because God favors those who are humble. It says this in Proverbs 3:34, "Toward the scorners he is scornful, but to the humble he gives favor."

Being humble is a choice. Choose to be humble: humble before God and humble before others.

DAILY DO

Talk with your parents about what it looks like to be humble. Ask your parents to tell you ways you can work on your humility.

DAY 25

"Jesus answered, 'I am the way and the truth and the life. No one comes to the Father except through me.'"

- John 14:6

DAILY DEVOTIONAL

We are entirely reliant on Jesus for our salvation. We only have access to God because of what Jesus has done. Jesus is the only way we can get to heaven. Jesus is the truth so many people search for. And Jesus is the only thing that can give life. Jesus tells us in John 10:10, "The thief comes to steal and kill and destroy, but I have come that you may have life and have it abundantly."

Many things in this world promise to give you satisfaction and fulfillment, but we know that only Jesus can bring satisfaction and fulfillment because of today's verse.

Matthew 6:19-20 says the following: "Do not lay up for yourselves treasures on earth, where moth and rust destroy and where thieves break in and steal, but lay up for yourselves treasures in heaven, where neither moth nor rust destroys and where thieves do not break in and steal."

Why would you put your hope and treasure in something that fades? The brand-new video game you bought only brings satisfaction for a little while, and then it fades, and you want the next latest game. Put your hope and your treasure in God, who will never fail you. In Hebrews 13:5, God states he "will never leave you nor forsake you." It would be much better to put your hope in God than anything else in this world.

DAY 25

Jesus is so important because he did what you and I could not do and paid the consequence that you and I deserve. You see, God is perfect, and man is sinful. God knows no sin, so a perfect God cannot be with imperfect sinners. In John 3:16, "God so loved the world, that he gave his only Son, that whoever believes in him should not perish but have eternal life." Jesus lived without sin, and "while we were still sinners, Christ died for us" (Romans 5:8).

Eternal life and hope are found in Jesus. There's nothing better to place your hope in.

DAILY DO

Pray for those who do not know Jesus yet as their Lord and Savior. Ask that the light of God will shine upon their hearts.

DAY 25 CHECK IN

DAY 26

"Don't be afraid because I am with you."

- Isaiah 43:5

DAILY DEVOTIONAL

Life can be scary. We can be scared of someone, something, or even the unknown. We have talked a lot about God in this devotional book, but not so much about the devil. The biggest lie you can ever believe is that the devil does not exist. The devil is real; there is spiritual warfare all around, but God tells us not to be afraid because he is with us. 1 Peter 5:8 tells us, "Our adversary, the devil, prowls around like a roaring lion seeking someone to devour."

There are two things that the devil can bring into our lives that God cannot: temptation and fear.

It says in James 1:13, "Let no one say when he is tempted, 'I am being tempted by God.' for God cannot be tempted with evil, and God tempts no one." So, it is proven God does not tempt us.

It also says in 2 Timothy 1:7, "For God gave us a spirit not of fear but of power and love and self-control." It is also proven that the Holy Spirit does not give us fear.

So anytime you're tempted or fearful, you know this is not from God but the devil.

However, fear and temptation are real things in our lives. So what are we to do when we are tempted and afraid? The answer is simple. You ask God for help. If you do not know how to do a math question in school, you ask your teacher for help. When you did not know how to tie your shoes, you asked your parents to help. So, the same is true for God. When tempted, ask God to give you the strength to resist temptation. When you are afraid, ask God to replace that fear with power, love, and self-control.

The two easiest ways to let go of fear are to:

1. Pray. Ask God for help.

2. Fill your heart with the love of God. 1 John 4:18 tells us, "There is no fear in love, but perfect love casts out fear."

Stay confident that the King of Kings is always with you. Remember that no one, no thing, and surely not even the devil can defeat God, so what is there to be afraid about? Through God, we have power.

DAILY DO

Whenever you get scared of anything, remember that the Lord has said, "Don't be afraid because I am with you," and truly believe that he is when you say it.

DAY 27

*"And we know that for those who love God,
all things work together for good."*

- Romans 8:28

DAILY DEVOTIONAL

Nothing just happens. Every event in life has a reason and purpose for occurring at the time it occurred. Every event is preparing you for a future event.

God does not produce evil. It is not in his nature. Only Satan and our sinful flesh can produce evil and sin. However, sometimes God will use the obstacles produced by evil to bring forth his good.

But no matter what the enemy does on earth, those who love God will never be victims because everything works together for good. Although problems may seem like they always surround us, we should not be afraid or have anxiety; God will always work things out in our favor. What may seem like a big problem now could become a big blessing.

DAILY DO

Memorize today's verse—only 15 words, yet it is so profound. Write it on your mind and on your heart.

"And we know that for those who love God, all things work together for good."

DAY 28

*"You will call my name. You will come to me
and pray to me. And I will listen to you."*

- Jeremiah 29:12

DAILY DEVOTIONAL

Jeremiah wrote this when the Israelites were in exile. The verse above is God promising Jeremiah and the exiles that he hears their cries. Just as God hears the Israelites' cries, he also hears yours. Just as God had the Israelites in mind 4000 years ago, he has you in mind today.

Don't hesitate to call out to God. You are already on his mind. He wants to help and bless you. In fact, Matthew 7:7-11 tells us, "Ask, and it will be given to you; seek and you will find: knock, and it will be opened to you. For everyone who asks receives, and the one who seeks finds, and to the one who knocks, it will be opened. Or which one of you, if his son asks him for bread, will give him a stone? Or if he asks for a fish, will give him a serpent? If you then, who are evil, know how to give good gifts to your children, how much more will your Father in heaven give good things to those who ask him!"

It also tells us in Philippians 4:6, "Do not be anxious about anything, but in everything by prayer and supplication with thanksgiving let your *requests be made known* to God."

DAILY DO

Let's practice making our requests known to God. Pray to him.

DAY 28

Cry out to him. Be honest with God and tell him how you feel. Tell him what you are going through. Tell him how you want him to help you.

DAY 29

*"So God created mankind in His own image,
in the image and likeness of God He created
him; male and female He created them."*

- Genesis 1:27

DAILY DEVOTIONAL

God created man and woman in his image and likeness. A man is a man, and a woman is a woman; there is no mix-up because God wanted to have balance and duality. God intentionally made the differences between a man and a woman. He created them to represent the various sides of his personality. That is why a man thinks and reacts differently from how a woman thinks and reacts to situations. Be proud that you were created as a man, and respect every woman you know and will ever meet. We are God's unique idea, an expression of his image and creativity. We are a beautiful work of art that he loves dearly. A woman is unique in her way, and a man is also unique in his way. Any idea about man and woman that isn't the same as God's idea is a lie.

DAILY DO

Thank God for his great idea of creating humanity and making you a part of his grand plan.

DAY 30

"Love your neighbor as yourself."

- Matthew 22:39

DAILY DEVOTIONAL

Ephesians 5:1 says, "Be imitators of God, as beloved children. And walk in love as Christ loved us."

1 John 4:7-8 says the following: "Beloved, let us love one another, for love is from God, and whoever loves has been born of God and knows God. Anyone who does not love does not know God because God is love." So, how are we to love others? The answers are in the passages of Scripture above:

1. We are to love others as we would love ourselves.

2. Imitate Jesus as best you can and live as he did.

3. Love others as God loves us.

When it says to love your neighbors, who is Jesus talking about? Your neighbors are not just the people living in the house next door but everyone you come in contact with. The same love you show to yourself, show to your next-door neighbor, show to your classmate, show to your mom and dad, show to your enemy.

It is easy to love those who love you. It is much harder to love those who do not. The Bible addresses this in Matthew 5:44, where Jesus tells us, "Love your enemies and pray for those who persecute you, so that you may be sons of your Father who is in heaven." Then, two verses later in Matthew 5:46, Jesus says, "For if you love those who love you, what reward do you have?

DAY 30

Do not even tax collectors do the same?"

There's nothing difficult about loving those who love you, but loving those who don't is much more challenging. When you love those who make fun of you and do not love you, that is when you are advancing the kingdom of God. When you love those who make fun of you and do not show love to you, you are loving others as you would yourself. You are imitating Jesus. You are loving others as God loves you.

God is love, and he lives in you. So, share God's love today.

DAILY DO

Do two things.

1. Tell someone who loves you that you love them and are thankful for them.
2. Invite the one person in your class who is not kind to you to hang out or spend the night at your house.

DAY 31

"If God is for us, who can be against us?"

- Romans 8:31

DAILY DEVOTIONAL

Have you ever played a game of pickup basketball or backyard football where you choose teams by captains? When you are a captain, you want to choose the best player. The one you think will give you the best chance of winning. Sometimes, the person we pick to be on our team is so good that they practically win the game for us. It's almost like the others are overpowered. Or, in your generation's terms: "O-P."

God is the greatest teammate we could ever ask for. To have him on our team guarantees us victory. There is no man, no obstacle, not even the devil could defeat God. God is undefeated and unconquerable. When God is for you, you do not have to worry about what life may bring your way because, with God by your side, he will carry you through anything that comes your way. How awesome is it that the God of the universe is on your side?

DAILY DO

Memorize the verse for today: "If God is for us, who can be against us?" Remember that you have the God of the universe on your side; with him, all things are possible.

DAY 32

" I sought the Lord, and he answered me and delivered me from all my fears. Those who look to him are radiant, and their faces shall never be ashamed."

- Psalm 34:4-5

DAILY DEVOTIONAL

Notice how David writes in this Psalm that he "sought the Lord." And because he sought the Lord, the Lord answered and delivered David from his fears. Let me ask you: what are you seeking? Are you truly all in for Jesus? Where is your time spent? What do you think about throughout the day?

David was known as a man after God's own heart. David sought God with all he had. Now, obviously, David was older and more mature than you are right now, but what's keeping you from being a man after God's own heart?

Jesus went all in for you, so we are to go all in for Jesus. When you seek God with your whole heart, he will answer you. He will deliver you. He will fill you up with the fullness of joy. As it says in Psalm 16:11, "You make known to me the path of life; in your presence, there is fullness of joy; at your right hand are pleasures forevermore."

When you look to God, today's verse says you will be radiant and will not be ashamed. Why would you ever not look to God and want what he has in store for you?

DAY 32

DAILY DO

1. Talk with your parents or someone you trust.
2. Tell them that you want to be *all in* for Jesus.
3. Ask them, "How do they go *all in* for Jesus?"
4. Learn from them, see how they seek the Lord, and see if you can apply that to your life.

DAY 33

"For God so loved the world, that he gave his only Son, that whoever believes in him should not perish but have an everlasting life."

- John 3:16

DAILY DEVOTIONAL

If you have ever struggled to understand the gospel or had difficulty explaining it, this verse simplifies it for you. This verse tells us that God sent his son, Jesus Christ, to die for us, saving us from sin and spiritual death. In the Old Testament, whenever people sinned, they would have to take a lamb and sacrifice it, and the blood of the lamb would atone for their sins. Jesus was sacrificed on our behalf, and his blood atones for our sins. That is why we call Jesus the Lamb of God.

We are deserving of death, but since Jesus suffered the death you and I deserve, we no longer have to. All we have to do is believe in him, and we will have eternal life. It is so simple yet so profoud. It is truly a simple gospel. God made salvation possible for us because he loves us. He loves you, your family, friends, teachers, and everyone else you can think of. He wants you to spend all of eternity with him in heaven.

DAILY DO

Listen to the song "Simple Gospel" by United Pursuit.

DAY 34

*"The Lord, your God, will go ahead of you.
He will fight for you."*

DAILY DEVOTIONAL

All throughout the Bible, we read and see stories of God showing up in miraculous ways to fight for his people in the Bible. One of these stories takes place in the Old Testament. The context in which this verse was written referred to the Israelites in slavery to Egypt. Throughout Exodus, we get to see the story of how God fought for the Israelites and eventually delivered them from slavery. In the story, God uses Moses to free the Israelites from their captivity in Egypt. In the verse from today, Deuteronomy 1:30, Moses reminds the Israelites that the Lord will go ahead of them and fight for them as he did in Egypt.

You see, just like us, the Israelites were quick to forget the incredible miracles and ways that God showed up for them. Despite God showing his goodness towards the Israelites by delivering them from slavery, the Israelites quickly turned their backs against God and sinned—a LOT. When God does something good for you, and you are quick to forget it, this hurts God every time.

Here's the takeaway from today's lesson: never forget what God did in your past, and be confident that God will always go ahead of you to fight your battles in the future. God is faithful to you, so be faithful to him!

DAY 34

DAILY DO

Pray to God now about any challenges you or your loved ones are facing. Tell him you trust him to fight every battle as he did for his people throughout the Bible.

DAY 35

"Tell your sins to each other. And pray for each other so you may be healed. The prayer from the heart of a man right with God has much power."

- James 5:16

DAILY DEVOTIONAL

The church is also known as the body of Christ. You see, when God builds something, he defends and preserves it. Back in Acts, God used Peter to build the church, and 2,000 years later, we still have the church. A common misconception about church is that it is a place or a building. The church is not the place or the building itself but rather the people in the building. The church was established so we can have communion with God and fellowship with other Christians. Ephesians 1:22-23 (NIV) describes it this way, "And God placed all things under [Jesus'] feet and appointed him to be head over everything for the church, which is his body, the fullness of him who fills everything in every way." In simplest terms, Jesus is the head of the church, and we believers are the body of the church.

One of the expectations of us as believers and the church's body is to pray for each other and encourage one another. If you ever feel convicted about something you have done, you can confess your sins to a leader in your church or another believer. This means you can confess to your youth pastor, small group leader, and parents to seek God's forgiveness and counsel from those wiser than you.

DAY 35

There is something powerful about confession and prayer over one another. It builds trust and "knits our hearts together in love, to reach all the riches of full assurance of understanding and the knowledge of God's mystery, which is Christ (Colossians 2:2)."

We so easily neglect the power of prayer and confession. They truly are significant. Prayer is a conversation with the Lord God Almighty. During prayer, you practice confession, acknowledging your sin and recognizing that you need to remove it from your life. Practicing these things will make you more intimate and become more like Christ.

DAILY DO

Choose someone you trust, a youth pastor, small group leader, or your parents, and confess some sins to them that you have not told anyone. Ask for them to pray over you.

DAY 36

"How can a young man keep his way pure?
By guarding it according to your word."

- Psalm 119:9

DAILY DEVOTIONAL

We are trying to live a pure, blameless, and sinless life. Of course, we can never reach perfection, but we should strive to be like Christ. If you ever have a question about what you should do in a particular situation, the best resource is to see what the Bible says.

Let's imagine you are playing on the Xbox, and you only have one controller, and your brother wants to play. But since you only have one controller, only one person can play. Obviously, the Bible does not explicitly say anything about sharing your Xbox controller because they did not have the Xbox back in Jesus' day. Still, the Bible does say in Matthew 7:12, "So whatever you wish others would do to you, do also to them." 2 Corinthians 9:7 says, "The Lord loves a cheerful giver." Luke 6:30 says, "Give to everyone who begs from you, and from the one who takes away your goods do not demand them back."

So, while none of these passages of Scripture ever say the word "Xbox" in them, they emphasize the importance of giving generously and sacrificially. In the case of playing Xbox with only one controller, if your brother asks you if he can play, you should stop playing and let him play the Xbox.

You can verify any act or choice with what Scripture says. God gave us his word to help us with our choices. Psalm 1:1-2

DAY 36

says, "Blessed is the man who walks not in the counsel of the wicked, nor stands in the way of sinners, nor sits in the seat of scoffers, but his delight is in the law of the Lord, and on his law he meditates day and night." We should depend on God's word. We should meditate on God's word. We should go to God's word when we have questions because it has all the answers.

DAILY DO

Read the first chapter of Psalm. Notice how it describes when a man meditates on God's word.

DAY 37

"Therefore, my beloved, flee from idolatry."

- 1 Corinthians 10:14

DAILY DEVOTIONAL

You may be asking, "What exactly is idolatry?" Idolatry is worshiping or loving anything more than God. If you love something so much that you become obsessed with it, the thing you have become obsessed with has become an idol you worship, and this hurts God's heart.

God must be the first in your heart above everything and anyone else because he is your creator and loves you more than anyone or anything else ever could. No one should take God's place in your life.

DAILY DO

Do a check of your heart today; is there something or someone that is becoming an idol to you?

DAY 38

"Therefore, if anyone is in Christ, he is a new creation."

- 2 Corinthians 5:17

DAILY DEVOTIONAL

Anyone who has given his life to Jesus shall be made into a new creation. He or she shall be washed clean from every sin and all guilt. Once you give your life to Christ, you are wiped of all debt that you owe. Sometimes, when we are in debt to someone else, we feel pressure and stress to make it up, but since Jesus is so gracious, you do not have to make it up to Jesus, nor is it possible for you to, but he forgives you of all the sins you have ever committed against him.

You no longer have to carry old debt, weight, and burdens because you have been made new in Christ. You can begin to grow daily when you study the word of God.

His word is like the food we eat. We eat food daily to stay alive and healthy. Just like we feed ourselves food, we must also feed ourselves the word of God. By feeding yourself the word of God, He will grow and develop you. He will make you a new creation. When you read your Bible, your nature and behavior change to be more like Jesus.

No matter how much sin you have committed or how far you feel from God, God can turn anyone into a new creation. God is ready to and wants to make everyone a new creation.

DAY 38

DAILY DO

Say this prayer, "Thank you, Lord, for saving my soul and making me a new creation. Amen."

DAY 39

"The thief comes to steal and kill and destroy. But I came that you may have life and have it abundantly."

-John 10:10

DAILY DEVOTIONAL

There are four ways you can live your life, but only one will give you abundant life. You can live:

1. From God—running away from God, hoping your sin will never catch up to you

2. Above God—not caring about what God has for you because you want to be the God of your own life

3. For God—doing good acts for God because you are trying to work your way into heaven

4. With God—living life daily with God. This is the only way that you will have abundant life.

We live in a world where so many live from, above, or for God; because of that, they have these never-ending highs and lows. They go through this constant cycle of a sweet season and a season where they feel sick of their shortcomings.

Ecclesiastes 1:2 says, "Vanity of vanities says the Preacher, vanity of vanities! All is vanity." In this context, vanity means "empty" or "meaningless." Solomon, the author of this book, is the "Preacher" it refers to in the verse. In the Old Testament,

DAY 39

preachers would preach in the part of the temple that they called the "Holy of Holies." Solomon is saying everything outside of this section of the temple is "vanity of vanities" and that "all is vanity" or "all is empty." Solomon is someone who had nearly everything the world had to offer—he was the wealthiest man ever to live. He is saying that life apart from God is meaningless and empty. If a man who had it all said that life is only abundant with God, why do we try to find life apart from God?

We should try to live with God because only in him will we have abundant life.

DAILY DO

Ask and talk with your mom and dad about what living with God looks like.

DAY 40

"Pray for all people. Ask God for the things people need, and be thankful to Him."

- 1 Timothy 2:1

DAILY DEVOTIONAL

We are called as Christians to pray for others. Not just those who love us but also those who persecute us. Matthew 5:44-45 says, "Love your enemies and pray for those who persecute you, so that they may be sons of your Father who is in heaven." It's a command from Jesus that we pray and pray fervently.

When Jesus was crucified, he prayed to God to forgive the men who nailed, flogged, and mocked him. Even though people were persecuting Jesus, he prayed for them. That is so selfless and amazing! Praying for others grows your selflessness.

DAILY DO

As you've learned today, pray for at least three people (you cannot be one of them), and 1 of those people has to be someone who "persecutes" you.

DAY 41

"The Lord is great. He is worthy of our praise."

- Psalm 145:3

DAILY DEVOTIONAL

God is the only being worthy of our praises. Only God is worthy of our praise because only God is capable of saving a man's soul from sin. Only God is capable of creating the entire world. Only God is capable of perfection.

Sometimes, we overpraise and glorify people here on earth. But the people we like to overpraise tend to change year after year, era after era. For example, there was once a band named the Beatles. From the 1960s to the 1970s, the Beatles were the biggest band in the world. They were the face of music. If you were to ask your grandparents, they would know who the Beatles were. Your grandparents probably listened to them often. Even if you asked your parents, they would know who the Beatles were. Your parents also probably listened to the Beatles, but I'm willing to bet that they did not listen to the Beatles as much as your grandparents. Now, let's look at you. Maybe you do know who the Beatles are, maybe you do not, but I am pretty confident you do not listen to their music or that you could not tell me the name of the Beatles' lead singer.

The point is that one of the most famous groups in the world is now a band that your generation does not even care about. The lead singer of the Beatles, whose name you did not know, is John Lennon. He once said, "We're more popular than Jesus now. I do not know what will go first–rock 'n roll or Christianity." John

DAY 41

Lennon said this in 1966. Fast forward to today. You did not even know who John Lennon was, nor did you even listen to the Beatles, but millions still gather on Sunday to praise God. Only God is capable of receiving everlasting praise. Let the words of your lips speak of the praises of God because only he is worthy of praise. How awesome and powerful he is that people praised him 4,000 years ago and still praise him today.

Praise the Lord! He alone is worthy of our praise!

DAILY DO

Choose your favorite worship song and sing praise to God. He delights in your praises.

DAY 42

"I know the plans I have in mind for you, declares the Lord; they are plans for peace, not disaster, to give you a future filled with hope."

- Jeremiah 29:11

DAILY DEVOTIONAL

Before God created you, he had you in his mind; he knew you and had a perfect plan written down for you. His plans are good because he has a hope-filled future for you. He wants the best for you, but the question is: Do you want God's plan?

God wants to teach you to be responsible, respectful, loving, kind, selfless, and faithful. He teaches you these attributes through the authority in your life: parents, teachers, and coaches. He teaches you these attributes through trials that test your faith. He teaches you these attributes by blessing you so that you may bless him.

Remember that God has a plan for you, and if you desire to walk in his plans for you, then you must remain faithful and obedient to him.

DAILY DO

Say this prayer, "Lord, I thank you for the plans you have for me. I submit to them today and for the rest of my life. So, help me, Lord, in Jesus' name. Amen."

DAY 43

"Jesus said, 'Let the little children come to me, and do not hinder them, for the kingdom of heaven belongs to such as these.'"

- Matthew 19:14

DAILY DEVOTIONAL

Children are very precious to Jesus. He was a great friend to them while he was on earth. He would lay his hand on their heads and bless them, and he still wants children to come to him now. He wants you to go to him; he wants to be your best friend. Imagine having a best friend that is Jesus.

Jesus said, "For the kingdom of Heaven belongs to such as these," talking about children. This means that anyone who wants to go to heaven must be like a child. We are to have a childlike faith. Kids easily believe what they are told – imagine back to your childhood days—if your dad promised to get you a gift, you would have believed him, right? It never occurred to you that he could fail to keep his promise; you were just excited to get the gift. This is the same faith God wants from all his children, kids, teens, and adults. Without faith, no one can please God. Keep trusting him for everything you need.

DAILY DO

Keep faith in God; know he is your best friend and will always have your back.

DAY 44

"Believe in the Lord Jesus Christ, and you will be saved."

- Acts 16:31

DAILY DEVOTIONAL

When Jesus was nailed to the cross, two criminals were also nailed to other crosses on his left and right. One of them mocked Jesus by saying, "Are you not the Christ? Save yourself and us!" The second man responds to the first criminal and says, "Do you not fear God since you are under the same sentence of condemnation? And we indeed justly, for we are receiving the due reward of our deeds; but [Jesus] has done nothing wrong." After this, he turns to Jesus and says, "Jesus, remember me when you come into your kingdom."

Jesus tells the man, "Truly I say to you, today you will be with me in paradise." You can read this story in Luke 23:39-43.

This is a beautiful picture because Jesus is reserving a spot in heaven for a criminal, proving that even the worst offenders can be saved if they believe in Jesus as the Son of God.

You believe in Jesus, and therefore, you are saved no matter what you have done. Your future is heaven. Hallelujah!

However, let me ask: if you genuinely believe that everyone will either go to heaven or hell and the difference between where they go is simply whether they believe in Jesus or not, what would you do? What should you do?

You should want to ensure everyone you know believes in Jesus so they can go to heaven. We are to share the gospel with

DAY 44

unsaved people and let Jesus work on their hearts so they can have a home in heaven. It will be an uncomfortable conversation, but it will be worth it.

DAILY DO

Tell someone you know about Jesus today.

DAY 45

"You are the light of the world. A city set on a hill cannot be hidden."

- Matthew 5:14

DAILY DEVOTIONAL

I want you to imagine a pitch-black room where you cannot see anything. The only thing that will fix that problem is light. Light is the only solution to darkness. Darkness cannot overcome the light because the light outshines the darkness.

We live in a world that is full of sin and darkness. The only thing that stands out from the sin and darkness is the light of Christ. When we have Jesus in us, we become the light of Christ. That is why Jesus calls you the light of the world. This world is in desperate need of help. This world cannot see how far they are from God because they are stuck in sin and darkness. We believers are to bring light upon darkness. By the light we shine, we will help others see Christ so that they can also be filled with the light of Christ.

DAILY DO

Be a light for someone you know. Talk to your parents about what it looks like to be a light.

DAY 46

"A fool doesn't like a father's instruction, but those who heed correction are mature."

- Proverbs 15:5

DAILY DEVOTIONAL

Why do you think your parents discipline and correct you?

It is because they love you and want you to grow into an incredible man of God. Just as your parents discipline and correct you because they love you, God disciplines and corrects you because he loves you. Proverbs 3:12 reads, "For the Lord reproves him whom he loves as a father the son in whom he delights."

More often than not, when you receive discipline or correction from your parents or God, they are trying to save you from making or repeating a terrible mistake in the future. Since both your parents and the Lord want what is best for you, you should give them your respect when they do correct you. When an adult corrects you, you should listen attentively and fix whatever they point out. Do not repeat the same mistakes over and over. Allow your mom, dad, coach, teacher, and God to correct you and speak truth into you so you can become mature, as today's verse says. To disrespect or disregard corrections from your parents is a sign of immaturity. As a young boy, I bet you want to grow into a man of God, and you do not want to be immature. So do what Proverbs 9:6 says: "Leave your foolish ways, and live and walk in the way of insight."

DAY 46

As a child of God, you must be humble enough to admit your wrongs and do things right whenever you are corrected. God is a Father, and he will always seek to correct you when you go on the wrong path. Allow him to so that you can become a mature man of God.

DAILY DO

Ask your mom or dad for areas of your life that you could improve in. Listen to what they have to say. Also, pray to God that he will reveal what you need to correct.

DAY 47

"I've commanded you to be brave and strong, haven't I? Don't be alarmed or terrified, because the Lord your God is with you wherever you go."

- Joshua 1:9

DAILY DEVOTIONAL

Joshua is a significant character in the Bible, especially in the Old Testament. God called Joshua to lead the Israelites to the Promised Land. This era of the Bible is known as "conquest" because Joshua and the Israelites are on a conquest/journey to take over the Promised Land. Before this journey, the Israelites were in captivity and slavery in Egypt for 400 years. Before Joshua led the conquest, there was turmoil and uncertainty amongst God's people since they had been through such a difficult time. Even while Joshua led the Israelites on the journey, many things caused tension amongst the Israelites.

We read in Joshua 7 that the Israelites lacked faith, and because of this, they lost a battle to the army of Ai, which set back the people of Israel's journey to the Promised Land. Amidst all the turmoil and setbacks, Joshua told his people not to be afraid because God was with them. We serve a God that gives us confidence. That gives us peace. That gives us strength. That gives us safety. Psalms 4:8 says, "In peace, I will both lie down and sleep; for you alone, O Lord, make me dwell in safety." This means that no matter what happens throughout the day and whatever is coming your way, you can be at peace when you go to sleep because your trust is in God. As you lay your head down on your pillow tonight, dwell in the safety of the Father, for nothing can stop our God.

Do not worry about the future. Jesus tells us in Matthew 6:34, "Therefore do not be anxious about tomorrow, for tomorrow will be anxious for itself. Sufficient for the day is its own trouble."

Take one day at a time and focus on what the Lord has for you

DAILY DO

Read Psalms 16:11, "You make known to me the path of life, in your presence there's fullness of joy, at your right hands are pleasures forevermore." Meditate on this and recognize that God has your back with whatever you are going through, and he will give you the fullness of joy.

DAY 48

"We walk by faith, not by sight."

- 2 Corinthians 5:7

DAILY DEVOTIONAL

In the same way a battery powers up a phone, faith powers us with energy.

Hebrews 11:1 says, "Now faith is the assurance of things hoped for, the conviction of things not seen." Faith gives us confidence and assurance. Everyone wants confidence and assurance but questions whether faith gives them confidence.

*This will be a short devotional because of what the Daily Do will ask you to do.

DAILY DO

Read Hebrews 11. Look at all the people who walked in faith and how their faith was rewarded. Everyone who walked in faith gained confidence and assurance.

DAY 49

"Christ's love is greater than any person can ever know."

- Ephesians 3:19

DAILY DEVOTIONAL

God's love knows no boundaries. He loves you more than you could possibly imagine. His love is so grand, so vast, so indescribable, so extravagant for you. Sometimes, this life can feel lonely, but there's no need to feel alone because God loves you and is by your side. Doesn't it encourage you that there's a God who knows your name and loves you so much?

DAILY DO

There is no love like that of Christ, who loved us while we were yet sinners. Listen to the song "Extravagant + Spontaneous" by MBL Worship. Recognize how much God loves you.

DAY 50

"Do all things without complaining and arguing."

- Philippians 2:14

DAILY DEVOTIONAL

Have you ever complained when something doesn't go how you want? Were you quick to voice your opinion? As a child of God, learn to listen more than you speak. God wants you to be at peace with everyone. We are called to be imitators of Christ and act as children deeply loved by him. Ephesians 5:1 says, "Therefore be imitators of Christ, as beloved children." To imitate someone means to act like someone. Sometimes, when we imitate people, we make fun of them, but here, when it says to imitate Christ, we want to become like Christ and treat others as Jesus did. You become more like Jesus when you make an effort to make peace with everyone. It tells us in Matthew 5:9, "Blessed are the peacemakers, for they shall be called sons of God." God desires us to live at peace with those around us. When we do that, he calls us his sons. Jesus did not strife with others and start arguments, so you should not do so either.

DAILY DO

Get a diary and write down the names of people and things you are grateful for. Practicing thankfulness is a great way to become a peacemaker. Then, write out the names of people you are struggling with. Talk to them today and ask for their forgiveness.

DAY 50
CHECK IN

> *"But why do you judge your brother? Or why do you show contempt for your brother? For we shall all stand before the judgment seat of Christ."*

- Romans 14:10

DAILY DEVOTIONAL

As a child of God, you are not to judge others because if you judge others, you are judging God's creation. God created and loves others just like he created and loves you, and who are we to judge God's creation?

As Christians, we are all God's children— we are a family. So, as a true family of Christ, God wants us to love, support, and respect each other. When others struggle with sin, call them out lovingly and pray for them. Do not harshly criticize them or embarrass them. Imagine if someone did that to you and how that would make you feel.

It tells us in Genesis 1:27 that we are created in the "image of God." We all have our differences with unique minds and abilities. Remember from DAY 9 that God is the greatest artist imaginable. He is the potter, and we are the clay. He is making something beautiful out of everyone, so do not judge others or what God can do through others.

It is easy to focus all our attention on the flaws of others and fail to see our own faults. We are called to remove the log from our eye before we look at the speck of our brother's eye. So do not judge anyone, and show respect to everyone, especially

DAY 51

with other Christians. Embrace one another. Even when you do not think you have much in common, you have one thing: the common bond, which is *Jesus Christ*.

DAILY DO

Appreciate everyone in your life for being different. That brings beauty into our world because God makes all things beautiful!

DAY 52

"Finally, be strong in the Lord and in his mighty power."

- Ephesians 6:10

DAILY DEVOTIONAL

As a Christian, you are part of the army of God; you are one of his soldiers, and he constantly trains you to be strong through your daily experiences. A soldier cannot go into the battleground feeling hungry and weak because he would be defeated. So, as a soldier of Christ, you are to feed on the word of God daily just as you consume physical food. We are to talk to God daily just as you talk to your best friend.

The word of God energizes and boosts your faith to fight every battle you are confronted with. It injects the mighty power of God inside of you. Praying to God gives you a tight, personal relationship with him. It changes your view of God from just this "big man upstairs" to a best friend.

DAILY DO

Read one chapter of Psalms of your choosing. Fill yourself with the mighty power of God. Then, listen to the song "Talking to Jesus" by Elevation Worship, Maverick City Music, and Brandon Lake. After listening to this song, pray and talk to Jesus yourself. Build your personal relationship with Jesus.

"Come to me, all who labor and are heavy laden, and I will give you rest."

- Matthew 11:28

DAILY DEVOTIONAL

Sometimes, our lives are so packed with responsibilities that the busyness of life gets to us. Our minds are constantly consumed with the question, "What do I need to do next?" Sometimes, our brains move a million miles per hour, and our soul is not up to speed with the craziness of life. Allow today to be a day where you stop, slow down, and let your soul catch up to your mind.

Finding authentic, genuine rest is essential because if you do not, you will burn out. After all, a car that drives non-stop and is never filled with gas will run out of gas. The same is true for you. If you go, go, and go, never slow down, find rest, and take the time to be filled up, you will just burn out.

How do we get filled up? Jesus, here in today's verse, says, "Come to me." So, if we want to find rest and get filled up, we need to go to Jesus, but what does going to Jesus look like? There are multiple ways you can go to Jesus to get rest:

1. Read your Bible (being filled up directly by God).

2. Close your eyes and listen to worship music. (If you fall asleep while doing so, that's OK! Just worship with a melodious heart for God).

3. Prayer (Be real with your conversation with God. Do not put on a show.)

4. Discipleship/Mentorship (Talk to trusted adults such as your mom or dad who love God and love you. Let them pour into their wisdom and care for you.)

DAILY DO

Choose one of these four things and do it. Whatever you have the greatest desire to do, do it now. Find rest in Jesus and be filled up by his spirit.

DAY 54

"Treat people in the same way that you want them to treat you."

- Luke 6:31

DAILY DEVOTIONAL

Our Lord Jesus commands us to be kind to others if we want them to be kind to us. Think of when someone did something nice for you—it felt really good, right? Now think again of something mean someone once did to you—you don't want to experience that again. Jesus knows this; that's why he wants his children to be kind to one another.

DAILY DO

From this moment forward, do something nice for people you meet, even when they don't do the same for you. Your act of kindness will change their hearts, and God will move in unexpected ways. Ephesians 6:7 says, "Whatever one sows, he will reap also."

DAY 55

"For you created my inmost being; you knit me together in my mother's womb. I praise you because I am fearfully and wonderfully made; your works are wonderful, I know that full well."

- Psalm 139:13

DAILY DEVOTIONAL

God made you exactly as he wanted you. When you were created, you were made in "Imago Dei," which means in the image of God. God gave you characteristics and qualities that display his image and nature through you. God's nature is being revealed to the world through you! How amazing that God chose to make you, just like we learned about all the way back in DAY 1. You were made with a purpose, so use the qualities he created you with to fulfill your purpose. That purpose is to glorify God.

DAILY DO

Write this somewhere where you will see it often (a journal, mirror, piece of paper by your bed, etc.): "I am fearfully and wonderfully made. God chose to make me the way that I am so that I could glorify him." Read over this note and think/reflect on it as you go throughout the day.

DAY 56

"Call to me in times of trouble. I will save you, and you will honor me."

- Psalm 50:15

DAILY DEVOTIONAL

There will be times in life that are more challenging than others. It is inevitable.

James 1:2-3 says, "Consider it all joy, my brothers, when you meet trials of various kinds, for you know that the testing of your faith produces steadfastness." So, we know God can use times of trouble and difficulties to develop you. Therefore, we should be joyful and hopeful when hard times come because they will grow us.

However, it is hard to have this mindset when the challenging moments come. We tend to complain, cry, or run away from the problem. But running away from our problems will never do anything about them. The Lord knows how hard it is to face the trials head-on, so he wants to help you. He tells you to call to him when those trials come so that he can deliver and develop you. God is dependable. He is the most reliable person you will ever know.

DAILY DO

Pray to the Lord and ask him for help with whatever trial you are going through. Look at the trial and see how the Lord will deliver and develop you through it.

DAY 57

"Whatever you do, work heartily, as for the Lord and not for men."

- Colossians 3:23

DAILY DEVOTIONAL

You are not the owner of your life, but you are the operator. Your life belongs to the Lord, and everything you do should be an attempt to give him glory. God gave you the responsibility to live your life in a manner that advances the kingdom of heaven.

View it this way: as a child, you belong to your parents. Until you are 18, everything you do is a reflection of your parents. Your words and actions can either bring praise to your family name or shame. We want to honor our parents and family name well, so we try to be obedient. But there are times when it is hard to be obedient. Sometimes, we will complain and grumble when asked to do something we don't want to. This is not how we should respond; instead, we should respond with a cheerful and joyful heart.

Not only are you a son of your parents, but you are a son of God. Your words and actions can either bring God glory or not.

Often, your parents, teachers, and coaches want you to work hard because they know it will make you a better student, athlete, friend, and person. So do not get angry and hate them for trying to shape you correctly. They only want what is best for you.

Similarly, God allows hard things to happen because he can grow you through them. God wants you to rejoice in hardship and to work hard in all that you do because it tells us in 1 Peter 5:10,

DAY 57

"After you have suffered a little while, the God of all grace, who has called you to his eternal glory in Christ, will himself restore, confirm, strengthen, and establish you."

You hear that? God uses your hard work to restore, confirm, strengthen, and establish you.

Take pride in knowing that you belong to God, and live your life in a manner that brings him glory. We are to work hard in all we do because it is a reflection of who Christ made us to be. By your hard work and good deeds, many others can come to know Christ. It tells us so in Matthew 5:16, "Let your light shine before others, that they may see your good works and give glory to your Father in heaven."

DAILY DO

Do all your work today, knowing you are doing it for the Lord.

> *"Do nothing out of selfish ambition or vain conceit. Rather, in humility value others above yourselves."*

- Philippians 2:3

DAILY DEVOTIONAL

As you have previously learned, Jesus lived a selfless life when he was on earth—he placed the interests of others before his own. Living a selfless life might seem hard sometimes, but remember, doing the right thing is not always easy. As humans, sometimes we desire to do things that God hates. That is our desire to sin.

My prayer for you is that you would submit to God's will and choose to follow his ways instead of your own. By doing so, you will become a lot closer to God. When we draw near to God, he draws near to us. This is because you are crucifying your sinful desires and doing the righteous will of the Father. This is not something you do once, but daily. There is a joy that is associated with obedience. I can testify that being obedient to Christ is *worth it*!

DAILY DO

Pray to God that when you have the urge to sin today, God will give you the discipline not to choose sin. Pray that God would help you crucify your sin and walk faithfully with him.

DAY 59

"This is the day the Lord has made; Let us rejoice and be glad in it."

- Psalm 118:24

DAILY DEVOTIONAL

You slept last night and awoke this morning, right? Of course, you did, which is why you can read this devotional. Never take the gift of life for granted. Never think this gift of waking up is ordinary because not everyone has that privilege/opportunity (Read Psalms 3:5, Psalms 4:8, and Psalms 127:2).

Each day is a day that the Lord has made, and you should rejoice and be glad in it. Give thanks to God every morning when you rise and receive his strength to carry out your activities for each day. You have the gift of life to live for God and bring glory to his name. You can do this by showing his love to others and growing your relationship with him. Don't waste a day. Live a life that brings him glory!

DAILY DO

See each day as an opportunity for God to express himself through you. Be grateful for each day. Now, go and live for Jesus!

"Don't let anyone look down on you because you are young, but set an example for the believers in speech, in conduct, in love, in faith, and in purity."

- 1 Timothy 4:12

DAILY DEVOTIONAL

Sometimes, as a kid, you may feel as if you have no influence, but I promise that as long as you are on this earth, you are making an impact. God made you to be a soldier for his kingdom to bring glory to his name.

There is a story in the book of Isaiah. When Isaiah heard the voice of God in Isaiah 6:8 saying, "Whom shall I send? Who will go for us?" Isaiah replied, "Here I am! Send me." Similar to Isaiah, we need to always be prepared for God to use us because whether you believe it or not, he will. He will use you to grow his kingdom. There are two simple steps that will prepare you to be used by God:

1. Be willing to let God use you.

2. Set an example for your friends and family in speech, conduct, love, faith, and purity.

By doing these two things, you are becoming more like Jesus. Others will notice the way you live, and they will say, "Oh, I want to be like (your name)." They are really saying I want to be more like Jesus because it is Jesus that lives through you. It tells us this in Galatians 2:20, "It is no longer I who lives, but Christ who lives in me."

DAY 60

DAILY DO

Think deeply about this. Are you setting a good example for other friends in your life? Are you being disrespectful and rebellious to authority? How can we fix that? Know that you are not too young to influence other people positively. Pray that the Lord will guide you in your choices to be an excellent example to others from today.

DAY 61

"If someone does wrong to you, forgive them. Forgive each other because the Lord forgave you."

- Colossians 3:13

DAILY DEVOTIONAL

Forgiveness is a crucial aspect of our walk as Christians. There will be times when you are wronged and hurt by people, but you should choose to forgive them because you have wronged and hurt God, and yet he forgives you. So who are we to hold grudges and not forgive others of their trespasses against us when we have so many trespasses against God that he forgives us of? To not forgive others after we have been forgiven would make us hypocrites.

God doesn't want us to strive with each other; instead, he wants us to show love through forgiveness and kindness. Not forgiving someone can drain the life out of you. When you stay angry for too long, it wears on you and affects your relationship with God.

God is too holy to hate or not forgive us, and if you have the Spirit of God in you, then you have the power to do the same. After all, you are a child of your Father.

DAILY DO

Is there anyone you need to forgive right now? Do that now. Pray to God that he would soften your heart to forgive them. Talk to that person and tell them they hurt you, but it is okay because you forgive them and want to be reconciled.

DAY 62

"Trust in the Lord forever, for the Lord God is an everlasting rock."

- Isaiah 26:4

DAILY DEVOTIONAL

I want you to think of a huge mountain or cliff purely made of rock. Imagine the Grand Canyon! Those kinds of rocks are hard to destroy. The rain, thunder, lightning, and floods cannot shake their foundation, move them, or wash them away. In the same way, God is like a rock. It even says in Matthew 7:24-25, "Everyone who hears these words of mine and does them will be like a wise man who built his house on the rock. And the rain fell, and the floods came, and the winds blew and beat on that house, but it did not fall because it had been founded on the rock."

It is great to read this devotional. It is great to go to church. It is great to read your Bible. But, if you are not applying the information you are learning from this book, church, or your Bible, Jesus refers to you as a foolish man who built his house on the sand. And when the rain fell, and the floods came, and the wind blew and beat against that house, it fell.

James 1:22-24 says, "But be doers of the word, and not hearers only, deceiving yourselves. For if anyone is a hearer of the word and not a doer, he is like a man who looks intently at his natural face in a mirror. For he looks at himself and goes away and at once forgets what he was like."

Build your foundation and your life on the everlasting rock of Jesus Christ. He is faithful, and you can always count on him.

DAY 62

DAILY DO

Listen to the song "Build My Life" by Housefires. Worship the Lord and be a doer of God's commands so your house will be built on the rock!

DAY 63

"People look at the outside of a person, but the Lord looks at the heart."

- 1 Samuel 16:7

DAILY DEVOTIONAL

This is so true! We are quick to form opinions and judgments based on what someone looks like, how athletic they are, how much "stuff" they have, how smart someone is, or what they have accomplished. We think that these things define a person, but the truth is they do not. God does not care about your worldly accolades or accomplishments. He cares about your heart. Don't get me wrong. Your worldly honors can bring God glory, but if you care more about your worldly accomplishments than you do about bringing God glory, that can be a heart problem.

Why do you do the things that you do? Why do you try to accomplish the things you try to accomplish? Is it so that you would receive glory? Or God?

DAILY DO

Talk and reflect with your parents about your intentions behind doing some of the things you do. Talk with them about how you can do those same things to glorify God.

DAY 64

"Our high priest is able to understand our weaknesses."

- Hebrews 4:15

DAILY DEVOTIONAL

Jesus Christ is our faithful high priest; he is seated at the right hand of God. Despite Jesus being God, there was a time when Jesus once lived on earth. So that means he is familiar with our human experience. This means Jesus perfectly understands what you and I go through. He knows how you feel when you get emotionally hurt or betrayed, or even little things such as having a headache, a wound, or a bump on your knee. Jesus faced everyday human life's trials just as you do. Jesus had a childhood just like you do. He had friends he laughed, cried, and played with.

Since Jesus, the Son of God, temporarily came as a human, he can sympathize with us. Jesus knows how it feels to fight sin and temptation, yet he never gave in at any point. He resisted every sin and remained holy all his life. That just shows how incredible Jesus is! How blessed are we to have a Savior like Jesus?

Sometimes, we feel people cannot relate to us because "they don't have it like we do." Maybe your life is more demanding in specific ways than your friend's. However, that is not the same with Jesus. Jesus can relate with you. I don't know if that encourages you, but it surely encourages me that I follow a Savior who can relate to me. It gives me some additional comfort and peace knowing that there really is a God who cares about me and you.

DAY 64

DAILY DO

Listen to the song "Son of Suffering" by Bethel Music. Recognize that there is a God who weeps and reaches for you.

DAY 65

"A new command I give you: Love one another. As I have loved you, so you must love one another."

- John 13:34

DAILY DEVOTIONAL

Everyone wants to be loved, even if some do not admit it. God created man out of love. God also created man for love. He loves everyone just as they are, and by his love, he seeks to save everyone from the bondage of sin. We are to love others because Christ first loved us.

A young boy named Chris always heard his pastor at church talk about the importance of showing love to people. So he decided to show love every chance he got. One day, while riding his bike on the street, he saw an older woman fall on the sidewalk, and she could not get up. For a moment, Chris looked away and kept riding because he did not want to deal with the inconvenience or awkwardness of helping the old lady. But the Holy Spirit reminded him of his pastor's words: "Show love to others as God shows love to you." Chris stopped and turned around to help the woman. The old lady was so happy that Chris had helped her, and Chris was delighted because she was happy. Chris felt a massive wave of joy and fulfillment on his way home. It sure pays to love others with the love of God.

DAY 65

DAILY DO

At a time when you would usually be annoyed with your friends, parents, or siblings, rather than lashing out in anger, show kindness and love. By showing them the love of Christ, it will encourage them to chase Christ.

DAY 66

"Jesus replied: 'Love the Lord your God with all your heart and with all your soul and with all your mind. This is the first and greatest commandment.' And the second is like it: 'Love your neighbor as yourself.'"

- Matthew 22:37-38

DAILY DEVOTIONAL

Jesus teaches us that there are two commandments from God that are the foundation of his other commandments. These two commandments are the greatest, and out of them come the other commandments, such as do not steal, do not kill, do not covet, and so on.

Why would these two be the greatest commandments? Well, if you love God with all your heart, soul, and mind, it will convict you when you disobey or displease him.

I would imagine you love your mom and your dad, and since you love your mom and your dad, you want to do things that make them happy, not sad. You wouldn't just randomly say something mean to your parents because you love them. This is because when you love someone, you will do your best to honor that person and bring a smile to their face.

This is the same for God. If we love God, we will do our best to honor him and bring a smile to his face. We bring a smile to his face by loving him and keeping his commandments. We also bring a smile to his face when we love others and treat them the way we would want to be treated.

DAY 66

DAILY DO

When you pray, don't just pray to God like he is "some big guy upstairs," but pray that you would love him and that you would be able to experience his love. Pray that you would love him with all your heart and that you could build your relationship with him.

DAY 67

"Let everything that has breath praise the Lord! Praise the Lord!"

- Psalm 150:6

DAILY DEVOTIONAL

God is worthy of all the praise we could give and more! Some of us fail to give God the praise he is worthy of. Did you know that in Revelation 4:8, at this exact point in time, there are angels in heaven that, "All day and night they never cease to say, 'Holy, holy, holy, is the Lord God Almighty, who was and is and is to come!'" The angels in heaven have been singing this since Jesus saved the world and will continue to sing it for all eternity. They never cease to say, "Holy, holy, holy is the Lord God Almighty!" They have been praising God for as long as time has existed, yet it is hard for us to be genuine in our worship for one song during church.

The Bible also says that rocks, oceans, and mountains praise the Lord. If these things can praise God, how much more can we humans, who are created in his image, praise him? God created you so that you could glorify him and give him praise. Praising God is not a responsibility—it is our purpose!

Praise and worship are powerful weapons that help us put God back on the throne of our hearts.

DAILY DO

Today, sing at least one worship song to God. This can be on the car radio, your headphones, or just aloud. Your worship will help you desire to serve and to adore God.

DAY 68

"I have no greater joy than to hear that my children are walking in the truth."

- 3 John 1:4

DAILY DEVOTIONAL

Walking in the truth means living according to God's word. It is essential to live as the child of God that you truly are. Live your life like it belongs to God because it does. Everything you have is solely a gift and a blessing from the Lord.

You are not alone because God is with you every step of the way. So do not live your life like an ordinary person who is trying to figure out life on their own. The Bible calls God the "author" (Hebrews 12:2). He is the one writing your story.

Have you seen an instructional manual before? It's that booklet that comes in the box with a new TV, video game player, refrigerator, etc. This manual gives guidelines about how to use that device the way the manufacturer intends for you to use it. If you choose to disobey or disregard these guidelines, then you are saying you know more than the manufacturer. Why would Apple say I can't put my phone in water? Because they know it will break if I use it outside their guidelines.

In the same way, the Bible was written as your manual for living on earth. It makes God smile when you follow his instruction manual because he knows you will have great joy and success when you do so.

DAILY DO

Study a passage of your choice from "God's manual."

DAY 69

*"Give thanks to the LORD, for he is good;
his love endures forever."*

- Psalm 107:1

DAILY DEVOTIONAL

Imagine that your mom or dad got you a Christmas gift, and you loved it but never said a simple "thank you." This would only discourage them from giving you another gift in the future. Whereas, when you express your gratitude, they are more likely to give you another gift in the future. Saying "thank you" to God shows that you acknowledge how good he has been to you. It shows that you recognize the love, mercy, and grace he is showing you.

God is worthy of our praise and our thanks. So praise him. Give thanks to him. When our mind begins to comprehend how much God loves us, our hearts begin to grow more and more grateful. Additionally, practicing gratitude changes your focus from what you don't have to what you do have. That will make for a happy heart.

DAILY DO

Thank God for being good to you and showing you his mercies daily. If you want to praise God with worship, listen to the song "Gratitude" by Brandon Lake.

DAY 70

"I can do all things through him who gives me strength."

- Philippians 4:13

DAILY DEVOTIONAL

Have you ever felt weak or not strong enough to do something? Maybe you've been scared you won't succeed. Yes, we've all been there.

Today's verse stands true because the strength of God is far greater than our own strength. Psalm 20:7-8 says, "Some trust in chariots and some in horses, but we trust in the name of the Lord our God. They collapse and fall, but we rise and stand upright." Many people put their faith and get the strength from their own power. The countries and armies in the Old Testament relied on the strength of their military, chariots, and horses, whereas David and the Israelites relied on strength from the Lord, and because of that, they rose and stood upright.

When the Bible says you can do all things through Christ, who gives you strength, it isn't saying that you will suddenly have a superpower to lift cars, houses, or mountains. It is simply pointing out that Jesus can strengthen you to handle every challenge you face because you have the joy and strength of the Lord in you. The strength of Jesus helps you to be content with what you have. That means you are always happy and satisfied with what your parents provide for you, without crying, complaining, and wanting what another kid has.

DAY 70

DAILY DO

Be satisfied with what your parents give you. Say a big "thank you" for everything your parents do for you. When things get tough, say to yourself, "I can be joyful and satisfied because Jesus gives me strength that is far greater than my own."

DAY 71

"Trust in the LORD with all your heart and lean not on your understanding; in all your ways submit to him, and he will make your paths straight."

- Proverbs 3:5-6

DAILY DEVOTIONAL

Would you agree with the statement that your parents know more than you? Yes? Why is this? Because they are older and wiser. If you should listen to your parents because they are wiser than you, how much more should you listen to God? If your parents know more than you and God knows even more than your parents, then God is a reliable source of instruction and wisdom. Do not misunderstand me. I am not telling you to not listen to your parents. Your parents correct and instruct you because they want what is best for you. You can learn so much from your parents' instruction. Just like with our parents, we also need to heed the instruction of God because just as your parents want what's best for you, God does too. His ways and instructions may be harder to follow, but they are better.

Matthew 7:13-14 says, "Enter by the narrow gate. For the gate is wide, and the way is easy that leads to destruction, and those who enter by it are many. For the gate is narrow and the way is hard that leads to life, and those who find it are few."

Those who lean on their own wisdom and understanding walk a path that leads to sin and destruction, but those who rely on the Lord's wisdom and knowledge will walk on a straight path that leads to life and life abundant.

DAY 71

DAILY DO

Listen and do the instruction of God. His way is better than your way.

DAY 72

"God is our refuge and strength, always ready to help in times of trouble."

- Psalm 46:1

DAILY DEVOTIONAL

God is your refuge and strength. He is always ready to help you in times of trouble. A refuge is a safe place, a haven, a shelter.

A great example in our current time of refuge is a refugee camp. This is a safe place where refugees hide from troubles or war going on in their country. Refugees are people seeking shelter from a foreign country. So, countries that are willing to help these people build refugee camps. In these camps, the refugees get a place to sleep, food, water, and every other essential thing they may need to survive.

God is so much better than a refugee camp; he's willing to protect anyone who comes to him, regardless of how close or far you feel from God or how much you have or have not sinned. God's arms are wide open to receive anyone who comes to him. People feel the need to "make themselves better" before they go to God, but God just wants you to come to him exactly as you are. God is a reliable refuge who strengthens anyone who comes to him, and he will wash away your sins and clothe you with a garment of holiness. Go to him exactly as you are, and let him do the work on you.

DAILY DO

Listen to the song "Where You Are" by Leeland. Tell the Lord that wherever he is, that is where you want to be.

DAY 73

"When people insult you because you follow Christ, you are blessed. You are blessed because the Spirit of God is with you."

- 1 Peter 4:14

DAILY DEVOTIONAL

As a Christian, you must expect persecution. Persecution can mean being insulted, ridiculed, mocked, outcasted, or made fun of. Matthew 5:10 addresses this and says, "Blessed are those who are persecuted for righteousness' sake, for theirs is the kingdom of heaven."

Jesus himself was mocked, insulted, and persecuted when he called himself the Son of God. So if Jesus, the Son of God, had to go through persecution, we also, as sons of God, would have to go through it.

Nowhere does the Bible ever promise you an easy life free of persecution. In fact, in Matthew 16:24, Jesus says, "If anyone would come after me, let him deny himself and take up his cross and follow me." Jesus tells you that if you desire to follow him, you must deny an easy life and be willing to suffer for Christ. Christ uses suffering to grow us. And 1 Peter 5:10 says, "And after you have suffered a little while, the God of all grace, who has called you to his eternal glory in Christ, will himself restore, confirm, strengthen, and establish you."

When you gave your life to Christ, you received his spirit. So, no matter what insult or persecution comes your way, don't be bothered because you have the Spirit of God in you.

DAY 73

DAILY DO

Say this prayer: "Lord, help me not to focus on the insults that others say to me. Please help me stay focused on you always and live a life following you. Amen."

"When we have the opportunity to help anyone, we should do it."

- Galatians 6:10

DAILY DEVOTIONAL

Something that is unbelievable to realize is that Jesus, the King of kings, came in the form of a servant to serve, not to be served. So if Jesus, the Son of God, finds joy in serving and helping others, you will also find joy in serving and helping others. Serving others can be done in a variety of ways. You can show love, or you can give someone something that they may need. Sometimes, all that someone may need is a shoulder to cry on, a warm hug, and a listening ear. Other times, you may see a homeless person on a street corner, and they may need money, food, or water. Think back to a time when you were served by someone else. What did it mean to you? How did it make you feel?

You do not have to do what is beyond you or give something you can't afford to give. But the little things you can offer are more than enough and can change a life. Do for one what you can't do for all.

DAILY DO

In the next 24 hours, go out of your way to serve someone and tell them how much God loves them. Do an act of kindness that helps someone out today.

DAY 75

"Let's not get tired of doing good, because in time we'll have a harvest if we don't give up."

- Galatians 6:9

DAILY DEVOTIONAL

Have you ever tried planting before? When a gardener plants sunflower seeds in the ground, he waters them daily and expects them to grow into sunflowers. But this growth does not happen in one, two, or even three days. Growth requires patience. It could take weeks, months, and sometimes even years to reap the harvest of whatever a person plants.

When you do good things, you are planting seeds, and you will reap your fruits when the time for harvest comes. God's message to you today is that you must not grow impatient or get tired of doing good because you are advancing the kingdom of heaven and glorifying God.

Sometimes, it looks like the good we do goes to waste, but God promises it does not. It says in Romans 8:18, "For I do not consider that our present sufferings are worth comparing to the future glory that will be revealed to us." Continue to do good, wait patiently, and reap the reward in the future.

DAILY DO

Say this prayer: "Lord Jesus, help me not to grow weary of doing good for your kingdom. Help me to plant good seeds in the lives of others so that they may come to know you. Teach me to be patient and wait to reap my harvest. Amen."

DAY 75
CHECK IN

DAY 76

"Because of the truth, which lives in us and will be with us forever."

- 2 John 1:2

DAILY DEVOTIONAL

Remember, from DAY 25 in John 14:6, Jesus said, "I am the way, the truth, and the life. No man comes to the Father except through me." So Jesus is the *truth*, and anyone who believes and accepts the *truth* will have the *truth* living inside of him.

Today's verse says that the *truth* will be with us forever, and the very next verse, 2 John 1:3, says, "Grace, mercy, and peace, will be with us." Because the truth is with us forever, so will grace, mercy, and peace. The fact of the matter is when you have the truth of Jesus in you, you have peace, you have joy, you have love, you have strength, and you have hope.

This truth dwells in us not just for a day, a month, a year, or ten years, but *forever*.

DAILY DO

Listen to the song "Fear is Not My Future" by Brandon Lake and Chandler Moore.

DAY 77

"Everyone who hears my words and obeys them is like a wise man who built his house on the rock."

- Matthew 7:24

DAILY DEVOTIONAL

Jesus told a story of a wise man and a foolish man who built houses. The wise man built his house upon a rock, while the foolish man built his house upon the sand. When rain fell, winds blew, and floods came, the house built upon the rock stood strong and never fell. But, the same weather came upon the house built on sand, and it fell. Jesus then said that everyone who hears his words and obeys them is just like the wise man who built his house on a rock.

The words of Jesus are the surest and strongest foundation that our lives should be built upon. That way, we will stand firm and unmovable when challenges, temptations, and hard trials come.

Take a look back at your life. I want you to refer to your life as a house. Has your house been standing upright, or has it fallen over and over again? If it has been standing, why do you think the house you live in keeps standing even after so many years? If your house keeps falling, why do you think your house falls when trials come? The answer is because of the foundation your house is built on. Any foundation that is not Jesus Christ is not a firm foundation, and it will fail. But Jesus Christ is a firm foundation, one that you can trust. What is your foundation being built on?

DAY 77

DAILY DO

Make Jesus Christ your foundation. Listen to the song "Firm Foundation" by Maverick City Music. Realize there is no better place to put your hope and trust in than Jesus.

DAY 78

"Why do you look at the small piece of wood in your brother's eye and do not see the big piece of wood in your own eye?"

- Matthew 7:3

DAILY DEVOTIONAL

Jesus used a perfect illustration here to describe how men judge one another. We are so quick to notice the faults in others that we will overlook our own faults. This makes us look like hypocrites. As Christians, we are to hold each other accountable, but it starts with holding ourselves accountable. Before you call out a brother who sins, make sure you are in the right standing to call him out.

Make sure you address your sins, faults, mistakes, and weaknesses before you tell another person to address theirs. Whenever Jesus was on the earth, there was a group of religious leaders called Pharisees. The Pharisees were the hypocrites that Jesus tells us not to be. The Pharisees were sinners, yet they often tried to judge other people because of their sins. Being a hypocrite displeases God and is why he tells us to look at and judge ourselves before judging others.

DAILY DO

Is there someone who constantly annoys you? Ask God to help you to be more patient, merciful, and understanding towards the person. Instead of judging the person, show them love just as Christ shows love to you even though you sin against him.

DAY 79

> "Jesus stretched out His hand and touched him, saying, 'I am willing; be cleansed.' And immediately, his leprosy was cleansed."

DAILY DEVOTIONAL

Sometimes, we have requests we want to bring to God, but then we ask ourselves, "Will God do this for me?" We fight so many thoughts that make us doubt whether God is willing to answer some kind of prayer. But the truth is, if it's something truly important to you, God will never turn a deaf ear to your request. This is not an excuse to ask God for unreasonable things; he can't give you what is against his plan for you or something you are not ready for. There is a perfect time for everything.

Jesus granted the request of the leprous man in the book of Mathew 8:3. The man was completely healed and made whole. His life changed forever. He received freedom through healing. When Jesus healed this man, people with leprosy had a skin disease without a cure. They were usually sent out of their homes and villages so they couldn't infect others. But, while most people avoided people with leprosy, Jesus went close to them. He touched them and healed them when they asked for his help. Jesus showed compassion for the sick. Jesus will not avoid you no matter how sick, sinful, or sad you are. Lean into him because he wants to lean into you.

Sometimes, we avoid God because we doubt whether he truly can help or heal us. But Matthew 17:20-21 says, "If you have the faith like a grain of a mustard seed, you will say to this mountain,

'Move from here to there,' and it will move, and nothing will be impossible for you."

Jesus is speaking to him in an exaggeration. You cannot physically move a mountain, but the reason you feel like God cannot help or answer your prayers is that you lack faith. We need to grow our faith in God. We need to have a dependence on God. Because everything is going to be alright, no matter what storm comes, God will hold you in his arms. God hears your cry, your deepest pain; he listens patiently, and he wants to help you, but you need to have faith that everything is going to be alright.

DAILY DO

Listen to the song "Gonna Be Alright" by Ryan Ellis. Pour out your heart to God. Have faith that God will lead your soul to perfect peace despite what storms you may be in.

"But he gave up his place with God and made himself nothing. He was born as a man and became like a servant."

- Philippians 2:7

DAILY DEVOTIONAL

This is a lesson we have touched on before, but it is so important that we need to go over it again.

Kings that rule on earth expect to be served, but Jesus Christ, the King of kings, did not come to be served but to serve others. (Refer to DAY 74 for reminder). If Jesus finds pleasure in serving others, so will we. We are to follow Christ's example for us on earth, and one of the best ways to do that is by serving others.

Matthew 7:12 says, "So whatever you wish that others would do to you, do also to them." It means treating others the way you want to be treated.

The Scripture above talks about the humility of Jesus, how such a mighty person gave up all his glory and majesty to die for us. Kings on earth are always hesitant to give up their power, yet King Jesus didn't think twice before making such a big sacrifice out of his love for you.

DAY 80

DAILY DO

Listen to the song "All Hail King Jesus" by Bethel Music. Listen to the lyrics and praise Jesus as the King and Savior of the world!

DAY 81

"Your Word is a lamp to my feet and a light to my path."

- Psalm 119:105

DAILY DEVOTIONAL

I want you to imagine yourself in a dark room. It is pitch black. It is so dark that if you were to put your hand in front of your face, you would not be able to see it. In a room without any light, it would be difficult to navigate or walk around the room because you cannot see where you are going. Walking into a room with no light can be scary because we cannot see what's around us. But all of a sudden, when a light switch turns on and we can see what's around us, we feel safe and secure.

Similarly, walking throughout life without reading your Bible is like walking into a room with no light. Going through life without reading your Bible can be scary because you aren't seeing how God is working. However, if you are reading your Bible, you are reminding yourself how great God is and how much he is capable of.

The Bible is the light for our lives and how God speaks to us. If you want to feel safe, secure, and loved by your heavenly Father, read the book he speaks to you through.

DAILY DO

Choose one of the Psalms to read. There are 150 of them. Read one chapter, think about it, and talk to someone about it.

DAY 82

*"Give thanks to the Lord because he is good.
God's faithful love lasts forever!"*

- Psalm 136:1

DAILY DEVOTIONAL

God deserves to be thanked through our prayers, praises, and worship because he is good, and his faithfulness lasts forever. God never leaves nor abandons his children. He has never failed anyone, and he won't start now. People can fail you, but God can't. It is not his nature or character.

In Psalm 5:2, David writes, "For to God do I pray." More often than not, when we pray, we are so full of requests that we think more about the request than being with God and in his presence. When you pray, worship, and give thanks, focus on how amazing God is. Focus on what he has done and what he is continuing to do. Focus on being in the presence of the God of the universe.

DAILY DO

Pray to God now. When you pray, focus on his attributes and why you love him. Thank him for all that you are thankful for. Pray from a place of sincerity, and quiet your heart before the Lord.

"Do not think you are better than you are."

- Romans 12:3

DAILY DEVOTIONAL

One of our world's greatest struggles is the struggle of pride. Pride can be defined as how much one thinks about oneself. Paul addresses the Romans in this verse 2,000 years ago because they struggled with pride. 2,000 years later, here we are in a world still dealing with the same issue.

It is good to have confidence in yourself and your abilities, but the moment you begin to think you are better than everyone around you or you do not need anyone's help, that is prideful.

Here's what Scripture says about pride in Proverbs 16:18: "Pride goes before destruction." This is where we get the famous saying, "Pride comes before the fall." To think you are perfect and do not need any help could not be farther from the truth. We all are imperfect, and we all need help.

Matthew 23:12 shares, "Whoever exalts himself will be humbled, and whoever humbles himself will be exalted." James 4:10 agrees with this and says, "Humble yourselves before the Lord, and he will exalt you."

When you recognize that you are not perfect, that you do need help, that you are not the god of your life, and that you humble yourself before God, you will then learn what it is like to have dependence and sufficiency in the Lord. We are all sinners in need of Jesus, so do not think of yourself better than others. We all have sinned and fallen short of God's glory.

We are all sinners in need of Jesus, so do not think of yourself better than others.

DAILY DO

Say this prayer: "Lord, I do not want to be arrogant. Teach me to be humble. Help me, Lord, and make my thoughts and conversations pleasing to you. Amen."

DAY 84

"And He healed many who were ill with various diseases, and cast out many demons."

- Mark 1:34

DAILY DEVOTIONAL

Jesus healed many people daily. Whenever he traveled to a town, which he did a lot, many people who were sick, lame, and demon-possessed were brought to him to be healed and freed. Jesus never turned them down because he had great love and compassion for them. Even when tired, he never stopped helping until his job was completed. He always put the needs of others before his—an act of love and selflessness that we should all work to imitate. That is, we must love and serve people in the best way we can, just as our Savior did.

DAILY DO

Do not avoid people, no matter how tired you are or how annoying they are. Love and make time for everyone just like Jesus loves and makes time for you.

Also, make time for Jesus in your day. Do you have a particular time in the day that you set aside to spend with God? Do you have a quiet time where you read your Bible? If you don't, set up a time and be faithful to it.

DAY 85

*"Children, obey your parents in everything,
for this pleases the Lord."*

- Colossians 3:20

DAILY DEVOTIONAL

The Bible commands children to obey their parents in all things. As long as you depend on your parents for all your needs, including the roof over your head, the food you eat, the clothes you wear, your school and medical expenses, and many other things you don't even know, they have the right to tell you what to do and what not to do. By being obedient to your parents, you are being obedient to God. So when your parents ask you to do your chores, do so without grumbling and be thankful for all that your parents do for you. This is the will of God for you, and he will be pleased when you obey.

DAILY DO

Your parents have sacrificed so much for you. Do something kind for them today. Tell them thank you, clean a part of the house for your mom that needs to be cleaned, or give your parents a big hug. Do something to show your parents you are thankful for them, and that will put a smile on Mom and Dad's faces.

> *"Do not let any unwholesome talk come out of your mouths, but only what is helpful for building others up according to their needs, that it may benefit those who listen."*

- Ephesians 4:29

DAILY DEVOTIONAL

What kind of words do you speak daily? Do you say words that are kind and uplifting or words that tear down? What kind of words are you repeating from your friends, TV, and music?

We are not to slander others or say bad words, but rather, our words are to glorify God. This can be hard to do. It tells us in James 3:7, "For every kind of beast and bird, of reptile and sea creature, can be tamed and has been tamed by mankind, but no human can tame the tongue. It is restless evil, full of deadly poison." It is crazy to realize that a body part so small can be so powerful and hard to control.

James 3:9-12 goes on to say, "With our tongues, we bless our Lord and Father, and with it, we curse people who are made in the likeness of God. From the same mouth comes blessing and cursing. My brothers, these things ought not to be so. Does a spring pour forth from the same opening both fresh and salt water? Can a fig tree bear olives, or a grapevine produce figs? Neither can a salt pond yield fresh water."

The words we speak are a reflection of our hearts because what comes out of us is often a reflection of what we put in ourselves. If you listen to music or TV shows that say bad words, you are more likely to say bad words. If you hang around friends who say mean things to other people, you are more likely to say mean things to other people.

So if you want to control your tongue, you need to surround yourself with input and people who speak things of righteousness.

The tongue is so powerful because, with it, we can say kind words that warm the hearts of others or bad words that cut and sting their heart. You don't wish to hurt or tear anyone down, right? So, speak good words to warm your heart and the hearts of others. Build up other people with your words by telling them things like, "Jesus loves you," "You are amazing," "You are so nice," and more that will bring smiles to their faces.

When you build people up with godly words, they will be more likely to see Jesus because they see his nature and character in

DAILY DO

Speak godly and positive words to your family, friends, neighbors, teachers, and everyone you come across today.

"And he who searches hearts knows what
is the mind of the Spirit because the Spirit
intercedes for the saints according to the will
of God."

- Romans 8:27

DAILY DEVOTIONAL

It can be difficult to fully understand the concept of the Holy
Spirit, but to make it simple, Romans 8:27 tells us, "The Spirit
intercedes for the saints according to the will of God." That
means that the Spirit intercedes for you. To intercede means "to
intervene or help on behalf of." So the Spirit helps you, and it
helps you in these six ways:

1. He makes you more like Jesus.

2. He gives you power to witness.

3. He guides you.

4. He convicts you of your sins.

5. He reveals God's word to you.

6. He brings you closer to other believers.

These six ways the Spirit intercedes can also be called
sanctification. Sanctification is the process of cleansing your
sinful human nature and becoming more holy. As Christians, our
goal is to become more Christ-like. That is what sanctification is.
The more Christ cleanses us, the more Christ is seen by others.

DAY 87

DAILY DO

Watch this video explaining the Holy Spirit by the *Bible Project*.

DAY 88

> *"Finally, brothers, whatever is true, whatever is honorable, whatever is just, whatever is pure, whatever is lovely, whatever is commendable, if there is any excellence, if there is anything worthy of praise, think about these things."*

- Philippians 4:8

DAILY DEVOTIONAL

Jesus only did things that were true, honorable, just, pure, lovely, commendable, and excellent. All these things are of God's character, and when we replicate them, it is attractive to God.

Philippians 2:5 tells us to "have the same mindset as Christ." When we do not have the same mindset as Christ, we are walking in sin, and when we walk in sin, that makes us feel farther from God. Sin is the separation between man and God; every time you choose sin over God, that is a small step away from God.

But there is good news: no matter how far you feel or how "separated" you are, God is waiting for you to return to him with open arms. So choose God over sin and make your mindset the same as Christ. Fill your mind with things that are true, honorable, just, pure, lovely, commendable, and excellent.

What you fill your mind with will most likely be the type of actions you display. If you have good thoughts, you will probably act in a God-honoring way. If you have evil and sinful thoughts, you will likely act in a sinful way. When sinful thoughts come into our minds that are not in line with the mindset of Christ, we are to cast them out.

DAY 88

DAILY DO

Pray that God would fill your mind and heart with things he is attracted to and remove anything that separates you from him.

"For all who are led by the Spirit of God are sons of God."

- Romans 8:14

DAILY DEVOTIONAL

I want us to read this verse in its proper context.

Romans 8:14-17: "For all who are led by the Spirit of God are sons of God. For you did not receive the spirit of slavery to fall back in fear, but you have received the Spirit of adoption as sons, by whom we cry 'Abba! Father!' The Spirit himself bears witness with our spirit that we are children of God, and if we are children, then we are heirs—heirs of God and fellow heirs with Christ, provided we suffer with him in order that we may also be glorified with him."

When you become a Christian, God grants you the Holy Spirit. This spirit that resides in you is the same spirit that lives in Jesus. How awesome is that?! Jesus was the Son of God, but since we have the same spirit that Jesus had, we can also be called sons of God! Romans 8:17 calls us "heirs of God and fellow heirs with Christ." Since we are now a part of God's family, it tells us that we will get to experience glory with God and Jesus.

To demonstrate how powerful the spirit inside of you is…

The spirit that's living inside your bones is the same spirit that:

- Raised Jesus from the dead (Luke 24)

- Allowed Jesus to do countless miracles (John 21:25)

- Created the whole universe (Genesis 1:2)

- Radically changed the heart of Paul (1 Timothy 1:12-20)

- Filled Bezalel with skill, intelligence, knowledge, and craftsmanship to build the Tabernacle of God (Exodus 35:30-31)

- Enraptured David with the love of God (Psalm 139:7)

And so much more!

That spirit that did all these things is now inside you. You are a son of God. Take pride in that. Be proud to be a son of the King and that you have the Holy Spirit inside you!

Lean on the Spirit for discernment, conviction, and correction. John 16:8 says, "And when [the Holy Spirit] comes, he will convict the world concerning sin and righteousness and judgment." The conviction you feel when you sin is the Holy Spirit trying to renew you and bring you back to the Father.

DAILY DO

Listen to the song "Rest on Us" by Maverick City Music. Ask God to allow the Holy Spirit to rest on your heart and fill you up!

"*Be kind and compassionate to one another, forgiving each other, just as in Christ Jesus forgave you.*"

- Ephesians 4:32

DAILY DEVOTIONAL

Forgiveness is extending grace to someone who has hurt you. We are to forgive others when they wrong us because we have wronged the God of the universe countless times, and he still forgave us. In the same way, God extends grace to you, he wants you to do the same with others—your family, friends, schoolmates, teachers, coaches, etc.

Matthew 6:14-15 says, "For if you forgive others their trespasses, your heavenly Father will also forgive you, but if you do not forgive others their trespasses, neither will your Father forgive you." Trespass here means sins, wrongs, or hurts. In this verse, it does sound like God's forgiveness for you is conditional, meaning you have to forgive to be forgiven. However, we know God already forgives you because today's verse tells us that Christ Jesus has forgiven us. More so, Matthew 6:14-15 is trying to say that as a Christian, you are expected to forgive others because you have been forgiven. You would be a hypocrite not to extend grace to someone else when God has extended you more grace than you even know.

The word "compassion" is the feeling you get when you see someone suffering or in pain and want to help them. Hebrews 4:15 states, "For we do not have a high priest who is unable to

DAY 90

sympathize with our weakness." Jesus showed empathy to others. Jesus showed kindness and compassion, and you can do the same.

DAILY DO

Do not hold any grudges against anyone who hurts you, but instead choose to forgive them.

---

*"All people have sinned and come short of
the glory of God."*

- Romans 3:23

DAILY DEVOTIONAL

We tend to think that some sin is worse than others, but in the eyes of God, all sin is equal because sin separates you from God. Sin is whenever you miss the mark, the standard, and the expectation of God. We have all missed the mark, so we are now sinful and imperfect. Since we are imperfect, we cannot exist with a perfect God. That was until a man named Jesus came to be the Savior of the world.

I'm not telling you the story of the gospel again; you already know it by now. Here's what I want you to get from today:

We all need Jesus. I don't care how righteous you think you are or how "little" sin you commit, you need Jesus just as much as the most sinful person you can think of. Do not think of yourself as better than anyone else because you think you are "less sinful." We all have sinned and fallen short of the standard of God. Recognize that everyone is in need of a Savior. Everyone needs to be sanctified. Everyone needs Jesus.

DAILY DO

Recognize you need Jesus just as much as everyone else. Thank Jesus for doing what you could not, and give him the praise he deserves.

DAY 92

"I am with you always, to the end of the age."

- Matthew 28:20

DAILY DEVOTIONAL

Life sometimes seems a lot easier to go through when you have someone with you—a friend to laugh with or a parent to cry to. But there will come times when no human can fill the void you are trying to fill. That is where God comes in. Matthew 28:20, the verse for today, is Jesus telling you that he will always be by your side. You never have to worry about a "void to fill" because, with Jesus, we experience the fullness of joy, contentment, and satisfaction. Also, notice how Jesus says, "to the end of the age." That means he is with you today, tomorrow, and the day after. Every second of every minute of every hour, God is with you. That means when the going gets tough, God has got you.

In the verses before Matthew 28:20, Jesus charges his disciples to spread the gospel to "all nations." That is something that is challenging and uncomfortable. As a Christian, you will go through hard and uncomfortable things, but the good news is Psalm 3:3 says, "But you, O Lord, are a shield about me, my glory, and the lifter of my head."

Jesus is *your* shield and *your* lifter of your head when the going gets tough.

DAY 92

DAILY DO

Pray this prayer to Jesus, "Thank you, Lord, for calling me according to your purpose. Help me to fulfill my destiny and make you proud. Be my shield when life gets hard, and please help me never lose sight of you. Amen."

> *"And he said, 'Come!' And Peter got out of
> the boat, and walked on the water and came
> toward Jesus."*

- Matthew 14:29

DAILY DEVOTIONAL

Yesterday, we talked about the importance of having faith. Having faith is so important that I want to share another example with you about having faith.

This story of the Bible represents the step of faith you should take as a believer in the middle of storms. In this story (which I encourage you to read in Matthew 14:22-33), the disciples are in a boat in the middle of a raging storm. The disciples fear for their lives. Then, they see a figure in the distance walking on the water. The disciples initially thought it was a ghost, but it was Jesus. When Jesus walks up to the boat, he reveals that it is him. Peter questions whether it really is Jesus, so Jesus calls him to step out of the boat. When Peter steps out of the boat, he begins to walk on the water with Jesus, but then Peter looks around at the winds, and Peter begins to sink before Jesus helps him out of the water.

The takeaway is once Peter took his focus off of Jesus and focused on the circumstances around him, he began to sink. When we take our focus off Jesus and look at the circumstances around us, it causes us to lose faith. Jesus even calls out Peter and says, "O (Peter) of little faith, why did you doubt?" Peter was literally walking on the water, yet he still lacked faith that Jesus would protect him from the storm. God provides so much for you and me, yet we still lack faith that he will provide for us in the future.

Today, Jesus is telling you to step out of your boat in faith. Forget your storms, fears, shame, pain, failures, and problems because God will carry you through.

DAILY DO

Why do you think you lack faith? Talk to your parents about it. Ask them how they have learned to have more faith in Jesus.

DAY 94

*"Rejoice in the Lord always; again, I will say
REJOICE!"*

- Philippians 4:4

DAILY DEVOTIONAL

The word "rejoice" is mentioned 183 times in the Bible. That's a lot! So it must be really important. The definition of rejoice is "to feel or show great delight."

Let me ask you. Do you genuinely rejoice in the gospel? God emphasizes that we are to rejoice in all that we do.

So, where does joy come from? Well, joy comes from God; It is an assurance in our hearts that God is good, sovereign, and perfect.

Psalm 16:11 states, "In [God's] presence there is fullness of joy." So, if joy only comes from the Lord, why do we try to find joy in worldly and material things? It is not wrong to have fun, play video games, or want presents for Christmas. But every year, you want new presents under the Christmas tree, you want the newest video game. Your Christmas presents and video games do not last forever. Only joy for the Lord lasts forever.

Sometimes, joy requires that you rejoice even in the face of tribulation. The Bible also says, "In all things, give thanks to God." So that means we rejoice in the highs and the lows. We need to give thanks to God every day. There are so many things we neglect and take for granted. You have a roof over your head, food on your table, and parents that love you. Give thanks to God and rejoice over those things.

DAY 94

DAILY DO

Make it a habit to rejoice and thank God daily for his blessings. Listen to the song "I'll Give Thanks" by Housefires.

God is more than enough. Why do you worry? Your God knows what you need.

Bonus Biblical Reference:
Matthew 7:31-33: "Therefore do not be anxious, saying, 'What shall we eat?' or 'What shall we drink?' or 'What shall we wear?' For the Gentiles seek after all these things, and your heavenly Father knows that you need them all. But seek first the kingdom of God and his righteousness, and all these things will be added to you."

"When I am afraid, I put my trust in you."

- Psalm 56:3

DAILY DEVOTIONAL

We all have different fears in life, but the Bible tells us that when we are afraid, we can count on God to help us out of it. There is nothing you are afraid of that God cannot handle. God constantly reminds us not to fear because he is with us.

In Psalm 56, David tells God that whenever he gets afraid—when his enemies surround him in a battle—he will put his trust in God. King David wrote this at a time when he fought many battles. Although David was a great warrior, he admitted that he often feared his battles.

Psalm 19 shares something similar. In Psalm 19:4, David writes, "The cords of death encompassed me; the torrents of destruction assailed me." This is David crying out to God that he is nervous because troubles surround him. But in Pslam 19:1-2 David declares, "I love you, O Lord, my strength. The Lord is my rock and my fortress, and my deliverer, my God, my rock in whom I take refuge, my shield, and the horn of my salvation, my stronghold." In Psalm 19, David declares that even though he is surrounded by fear, God is his stronghold and deliverer. At this point, David had enemies who were trying to kill him, but we see God deliver David from his enemies and King Saul.

The Lord was always faithful and came through for King David because David trusted God's faithfulness. A man who trusts God will see the faithfulness of God.

DAILY DO

Tell God now about anything you seem to be afraid of, no matter how big or small; tell him. Surrender fears to him, and begin to trust him to deliver you from them all.

"Do not forget to do good to others. And share with them what you have."

- Hebrews 13:16

DAILY DEVOTIONAL

When you have Jesus as the Savior of your life, you have the greatest gift of all time. We have a gift within us that makes all other gifts look like scum. 2 Corinthians 4:7 reads, "But we have this treasure in jars of clay, to show that the surpassing power belongs to God and not to us." Paul is referring to you and me as jars of clay compared to the treasure of the gospel that we have. How selfish would it be of us not to share that treasure with others?

The Bible says in 2 Corinthians 9:7, "God loves a cheerful giver." Give others a piece of the gospel by telling them about it or letting your actions reflect the light of Christ. Matthew 5:14 says, "You are the light of the world." And it goes on to say in Matthew 5:16, "Let your light shine before others, so that they may see your good works and give glory to your Father who is in heaven." We have a gift within us, and we need to share it with others.

DAILY DO

Is there anyone you know who needs your help with something? Maybe someone you know just needs a friend to hang out with? Maybe your classmate needs a new pair of tennis shoes? Talk to your parents and come up with a plan so that you can help that person.

DAY 97

*"Keep your heart with all diligence, for out of
it springs the issues of life"*

- Proverbs 4:23

DAILY DEVOTIONAL

Your heart is like a river that contains everything that flows out
of your life: your words, thoughts, and actions are the results
of what your heart contains. When Proverbs says to "keep
your heart with all diligence," this means to guard your heart
diligently. This means you need to be extra careful of what you
allow into your heart. Don't listen to or believe negative things
you hear about yourself; don't allow hate in your heart; don't
allow sinful influence to overtake your mind or heart. Do not say
bad words or gossip, for they corrupt your mind and heart.

Whatever a man cares about will become his treasure. And where
his treasure is, his heart will be also. It tells us so in Matthew
6:21: "For where your treasure is, there your heart will be also."
Whatever is in a man's heart will eventually control his life.
Therefore, let the word of God dwell in your heart and take
control. Allow nothing else but God's ways to be what your heart
desires. And you will find the life of God flowing marvelously in
and around you.

DAY 97

DAILY DO

Get two sheets of paper. On the first sheet of paper, write down the characteristics of Jesus and other godly things you can think of. On the other sheet, write all the sins and bad things you have thought of in the last few days. Crumple up the second paper and throw it away. No longer let those evil and corrupt thoughts corrupt your mind or heart. Fill your mind with heavenly things.

DAY 98

- Matthew 20:28

DAILY DEVOTIONAL

This is a verse I have used numerous times throughout this devotional book. Jesus came here with a purpose: to serve and lay his life down for the world so that we could have salvation.

Jesus had a ministry and mission to fulfill, and he did not let anything stray him away from his mission. Jesus did not chase after power, fame, or money. He kept his ministry as his central focus. Just as Jesus had his mission to fulfill, you have a mission to fulfill.

A ministry is not necessarily a church mission trip. It's your act of service that advances the kingdom of God on earth. It's whatever you do for God to spread the gospel so we can draw more people into the kingdom of God. A genuine minister does not do ministry for selfish gain but for God to be glorified.

DAILY DO

Let your life be an act of service to God. God sent you here for a reason. It was for you to glorify God. Go live your life on a mission for God!

DAY 99

> *"When Jesus spoke again to the people, he said, 'I am the light of the world. Whoever follows me will never walk in darkness, but will have the light of life.'"*

- John 8:12

DAILY DEVOTIONAL

When you have dirty clothes, what do you do? You wash them so you can have clean clothes. When you walk into a dark room, what do you do? You turn the lights on so you can see. You want to have clean clothes and see in a dark room so that you can live in an orderly way. If you have dirty clothes, you will feel messy. If you can't see in a dark room, you will become nervous because of uncertainty. We, as humans, desire order and certainty.

To follow Jesus is to walk in order and with certainty. If you follow Jesus, he will make you clean so you can live orderly. If you follow Jesus, he will give you light so you can see in a dark world and have certainty.

DAILY DO

Declare this today, "Jesus lives in me, so his light dwells in me. I am a child of light, and darkness has no place around me."

"He is not here, He is risen!"

- Matthew 28:6

DAILY DEVOTIONAL

The days after Jesus died and was buried in a tomb, his friend, Mary Magdalene, and his mother, Mary, went to check where he had been buried. Suddenly, there was a great earthquake, and the angel of God came down from heaven, rolled away the stone that covered Jesus' tomb, and sat on it. Then the angel said to them in Matthew 28:5-6, "Do not be afraid, for I know you seek for Jesus who was crucified. He is not here, he is risen." The two women were surprised, so they ran joyfully to tell the disciples of Jesus what the angel said.

Although Jesus died a painful death, he rose after just three days. How incredible a God we serve! We serve a God who has power over death. The enemy, Satan's, greatest scare tactic is to put the fear of death into people, but our God has defeated death and made the enemy's greatest weapon rubbish.

To us Christians, the resurrection of Jesus means everything. It proves that we have a Savior who is alive in heaven. He is God. He rose for you and me! And he lives forevermore! And since he lives, we are to tell others about him. Jesus says in Matthew 28:19, "Go therefore and make disciples of all nations."

We serve a God who is powerful and who laid his life down for you. That same God commands you to tell others about him, so do so! To keep the gospel to yourself is selfish. Therefore, we are to go and tell others about Jesus so that we can make heaven crowded!

DAILY DO

Tell someone the gospel or about Jesus today.

DAY 100
CHECK IN

THANK
YOU

Made in the USA
Coppell, TX
26 May 2025

49882885R00094